I0176841

How to Go From a Hot, Single Mess to Ready for God's Best

Written and Published By Afi Pittman

Cover Design By Tyora Moody

How to Go From a Hot, Single Mess to Ready for God's Best

Copyright © 2014 by Afi Pittman, Author of Faith
Enterprises

All rights reserved

http://www.authorofmyfaith.com

Thank you...to God for changing my life through a special encounter with Him while reading Isaiah 30. To Tyora Moody for an awesome book cover. To Marc Medley, Nicole Cleveland, and Lisa Coleman for interviewing me about the book and my single life. To Vanessa Richardson and Jill Monaco for asking me to be a guest contributor to their magazines. To my mother, Barbara Rutledge, for her support in everything that I do. To my sister-friend, Sonja Bronner, for encouraging me to be all that God has created me to be. To my mentor, Connie Turner, for opening my eyes to my own desire for marriage. To my current church home New Life Providence for making life in Hampton Roads, Virginia, a little slice of Heaven on Earth. To Miss Nancy Blalock for being a prayer warrior and a valiant example of what God does with women who stand for Him in this life.

This book is for...every woman who, after pouring her heart out about frustrations over singleness and waiting for a godly husband, was told, "Well, maybe you just have the gift of singleness"...or some similarly awkward response.

Why am I writing this book?

Well, I didn't *want to write this book...*

But I've heard that your ministry often comes from your pain. If that's true, I know I'm qualified to write a book about why some women stay in extended single seasons when they could in fact be married. After years of being brokenhearted, confused and angry over my own singleness, I finally had a life-changing experience with God that taught me the truth about Him, my life, and myself. It taught me some lessons about love, romance, marriage, and even sex. And now, I have a call and charge to talk about the painful reasons for those extended single seasons: faulty beliefs, closed and broken hearts, and yes – even God's will for us to remain single for those extended seasons. For whatever the reason, it's heartbreaking to remain single when at the end of the day, you really want to be married and you can't understand why you're still single – after you've done all you know how to do in dating, love and relationships.

But at the end of that heartbreak, you will stay stuck if you don't decide to have something new and align your behavior accordingly.

And so here we are, my beloved sister in Christ...

I know you're already an amazing person. You probably have a job you love or are at least good at, friends and family who love you, or are involved in your surrounding community in some way. But when it comes to love, dating, and romance, you're stuck. Maybe you're wondering why it's so hard to find a good man. Or maybe you're reluctant to believe that marriage is possible for you. Whatever it is, if you are tired of making the same mistakes and falling into the same pitfalls over and over in dating, love, and romance, you want to become an even better version of you, and you want to meet the right man and get married, this is the book for you.

This isn't a book that will show you how to how to "find a man." It's a book that will show you the truth about dating and getting married God's way. It's a book that will show you how to uncover who you really are, start the healing process for any old wounds, and to become a single, happy you who will attract the right kind of men – men who love God, will marry you, and will be accountable husbands and fathers. Throughout this book I'll share lessons I've learned about dating and preparing for marriage so that you can get ready for the love you truly desire – from God first, then from a man that God would entrust you to.

I'm sharing these lessons because I was a hot, single mess! I had no biblical dating know-how; I was listening to the wrong people; I wasted time on the wrong men, and then had the nerve to believe God was holding out on me. But I had an encounter with Him (that I'll share in a later chapter) that changed my life, my view of marriage and my view of Him. He showed me that getting married was only the start of fulfilling the original call of Adam and Eve to be fruitful and multiply. He showed me that even if He gave me my heart's desire – which was a good desire – it wouldn't have been good for me, because He needed to teach me what marriage was really all about. If you're ready to learn how to date God's way (which was designed to lead to marriage), prepare yourself for marriage, and strengthen your faith and contentment in God while you wait, you picked up the right book.

I truly believe in my heart and spirit that God longs to raise up a generation of adults and young adults who are strong women and men who yield strong, godly marriages, families, and communities. And that starts with you! So if you're ready to shake off the "Mr. Wrongs," old wounds, or shameful mistakes, get ready...It's time to go from a "hot, single mess" to "ready for God's best"!

Chapter Guide:

Part I: Discovering the Truth About Romantic Love, Dating and Sex...According to the Word of God

Chapter 1: Let's Get Down to the Truth About Finding Mr. Right

Chapter 2: Why You're a Hot, Single Mess

Chapter 3: What Are Your Motives for Wanting Marriage?

Chapter 4: What Mrs. Proverbs 31 Can Teach Us About Being Ready for Marriage

Chapter 5: Fundamental Truths About Sex, Love, Dating, Marriage, and Romance

Part II: Now It's Time to Work On You

Chapter 6: Truly Knowing God Will Change You

Chapter 7: Recovering and Rediscovering Your Femininity in a "Man's World"

Chapter 8: Marriage-Minded Men Do Pursue Women

Chapter 9: Contentment...The Perfume That the Right Man Will *Never* Forget

Chapter 10: A Special Word for Wounded Singles

Part III: Build Your Dating Life To Please God and Marry His Best!

Chapter 11: You Become Who You Hang Out With

Chapter 12: The Categories and Types of Men You'll Meet While Dating

Part I: Discovering the Truth About Romantic Love, Dating and Sex...According to God

All of the chapters in this part of the book are designed to give you a baseline from which we will operate while we talk about everything related to dating, courting, and preparation for marriage. They're also designed to help you see what the Bible actually says about sex, relating to the opposite sex, and your identity as a woman. Before I get to the part of this book where we talk about dating, I want to cover some key and fundamental truths about sex, love, romance, and marriage. By the time you finish reading this part of the book, you'll be able to figure out your current beliefs about sex, love, romance, and marriage, and replace them (if necessary) with God's truth about them.

Chapter 1: Let's Get Down To The Truth About Finding Mr. Right...

I used to think the term "Mr. Right" was so cliché. But now I actually kind of like it! I mean, if you think about the other words that could have been chosen to describe the man of our dreams, "Mr. Right" is actually a pretty good phrase for women all over the world. We could have chosen something like "Mr. Perfect" or "Mr. Everything," but we didn't. We said we want the **right** man, flaws and all, to walk beside us on this journey where faith and life collide.

But perhaps we sometimes get Mr. Right confused with something he really is not. And maybe this is why he seems so elusive. Maybe it's why we keep ending up with Mr. Wrong...over and over again. Or maybe we're unaware of the fact that God really does want men to pursue us! I know you probably can't tell by the way women and men sometimes conduct themselves, but it's true. God wants men to pursue us. He wants women to be secure in who they are so that they don't feel desperate to have something that ultimately will not make them whole. He wants the same thing for our brothers in Christ, but my beloved sister, this book is about us!

So let's talk about the truth about finding this elusive, seemingly mythical Mr. Right.

Mr. Right Will Find You

You might be familiar with the scripture "He who finds a wife, finds a good thing." (Proverbs 18:22) We know what many of our pastors, elders, and singles ministry leaders say...this means that Mr. Right does the finding! But I feel like so many single women – especially single, Christian women – just do not believe this. And I get it. We're too busy wondering "How are the men going to find us **when there are none**?" But I've got a special report for you. To hear it, go here: http://goo.gl/umREIz.

Now that you've heard the report, I want you to accept that it could very well be true. It could very well be true that there are more never-married men than women and that the ratio goes even higher for Christians! I know – I'm skeptical about research, findings and statistics too. But if you think about it, these statistics fall in line with the Word of God! Jesus fed a multitude of 5,000 people with 2 fish and 5 loaves of bread. Through God's power, Elisha had a widow with nothing to her name and nothing stocked in her house fill jars full of oil to the point that she not only paid off her debts but had some left over to sell! God can make something out of nothing. He can create abundance from lack!

And look, in Proverbs 31, the question is "Who can find a virtuous wife?" I find it interesting that it indicates that it's hard for a man to find a virtuous, good, godly wife. But it builds my case that the Mr. Rights of the world are looking for that right woman, just like you're trying to figure out why there are NO men on your radar! So be encouraged. Mr. Right is out there and if you are ready, he will find you.

Mr. Right is not a unicorn

Psalm 118: 8, NLT: "It is better to take refuge in the LORD than to trust in people."

I'm an active duty Naval Officer, and one of the things I love about the Navy is the colorful language used in day-to-day Navy life. One term is "unicorn", which is code for someone (especially a leader) who is supposedly a part of the team but you can't tell that by his or her absenteeism. A mythical creature that only a few know whether or not it really exists.

Ladies, Mr. Right is not a unicorn! He actually exists. How do I know? Because of all the reports from my sisters in Christ who were once just like you and me – once single (happy or miserable) – and are now happily married. Although I haven't met mine yet, I know that if it's God's will...my Mr. Right exists!

But an actual unicorn in the context of our conversation would be a man we've constructed in our minds who meets standards that – at the end of the day – just don't have any bearing on a godly marriage. So don't fall into that trap of making the infamous list of qualities that are full of preferences. Don't fall into the trap of forming an idol in your heart. For a new way to go about making your "list" and to avoid fantasizing about a unicorn, there's an exercise for you in one of the later chapters that covers how to build a list that will actually help you lay the foundation for a godly marriage. I really want you to get this right so you can avoid the mistake I made of holding out for a list of preferences. I want you to know what qualities and character traits you really need in a man, not just the preferences you feel entitled to. I also want you to learn that you should have the character traits you desire. Above all, I want you to desire marriage with a flesh and blood man, not a god you idolize and place above God.

Mr. Right Is The Lucky One

Proverbs 18: 22, NLT: "The man who finds a wife finds a treasure, and he receives favor from the LORD."

You're blessed to find a man who loves and wants to commit to you forever, but I really want you to understand that he's just as blessed to have you. Proverbs 18:22 says that when a man finds a wife, not only does he find something good, but he receives favor from God. In other words, Mr. Right will do well to marry you! You add a blessing to his life that is immeasurable. So much so that God gives him favor. You add a worth that doesn't even compare to the most valuable and rare jewels. Yes, when you find and marry Mr. Right, you should rejoice that God has brought this wonderful man into your life. But, Mr. Right will be thanking God for YOU!

Mr. Right Will Honor You

1 Timothy 5: 2, NLT: "Treat older women as you would your mother, and treat younger women with all purity as you would your own sisters

He doesn't have to believe, worship or study the Word the way you do. He doesn't have to even need to have the same thought process as you. He will, however, honor you in the process of dating, moving into engagement and then committing to marriage. To honor someone means to respect their person, their beliefs and their standards. But guess what? As a woman who is on this journey of learning and living by God's standards, you're not holding Mr. Right to standards God never designed. Therefore, Mr. Right will understand God's standards, respect them and respect you.

Mr. Right Will Be Imperfect

Ephesians 2:9, NLT: "Salvation is not a reward for the good things we have done, so none of us can boast about it."

Just like you, Mr. Right will have flaws and shortcomings. It doesn't mean he's not good enough to be your husband. It means that – just like you – he's a human being. Don't cut him off at the pass before he even has the chance to win you over by deciding his flaws mean that he's not worth your time. And don't put him on a pedestal only to decide later on that he's a monster because you romanticized away his flaws. A pedestal is not a position any human being was meant to be placed in. God is the only one who cannot fail. We are limited and our attempts at perfection are as well. To embrace our imperfections along with Mr. Right's, we learn to rely more on God to be the glue that keeps the relationship and eventually the marriage together.

Mr. Right Will Love God Above All

Exodus 34:14, NLT : "You must worship no other gods, for the LORD, whose very name is Jealous, is a God who is jealous about his relationship with you."

This means that he loves God more than you, his career, or anything else good in his life. To be able to put and keep God first is an ability you want your Mr. Right to have because when he puts and keeps God first, it's easier for him to keep you right where God wants you – second to only Him!

Mr. Right Wants to Be Faithful

Proverbs 5:15, NLT: "Drink water from your own well—share your love only with your wife."

Mr. Right understands the power of being a one-woman man. Therefore, he doesn't have an agenda to have you in addition to any other woman who catches his eye. He wants to be with one woman – so help him God! I've heard so many women question whether men are just wired to be unfaithful. Honestly, I think both women and men have natural the tendency to be unfaithful because we are all sinners. I think we act on it when we don't understand what's at stake when we are unfaithful. Even still, Mr. Right will understand the value of being faithful. After all, God made Adam to be with Eve, not Eve, Sarah, Rhonda, Karen, Tracy, Katrina...and whoever else comes along!

My beloved sister, if you don't remember anything I tell you about Mr. Right, remember this. He is real and he will find you if you are prepared!

Chapter 2: Why You're a "Hot, Single Mess"

So now that you know a little more about Mr. Right, let's talk about you. By now you should be asking, "Who are you to tell me anything, Afi? After all, you're still single!" And thank you for asking! In fact, it's the same thing I said to God and the mentor He placed in my life to water the seed of ministering to other single women about their pains and concerns over singleness. I said "What could I possibly tell another single woman about actually preparing for marriage God's way"? But God taught me valuable lessons directly from His Word and His communication with me. So I'd love to take this opportunity to tell you who I am and how I can help you.

I'm a flesh and blood woman with a heart full of desires that I believe God will fulfill. One desire is to marry God's way. I haven't lost faith that He can do it because He's literally made other dreams I had come true. But regarding my being single, I remember once asking God a question. It was around 2007 or 2008, and I was stationed in Norfolk and living in Virginia Beach. I was Christmas shopping in one of the malls in Virginia Beach and all of a sudden it hit me how much I would have loved to be Christmas shopping for my husband and children. So I asked God why I had to still be single. His response—which came as a thought I couldn't have come up on my own—was "Because when you marry, you'll never forget what it was like to be single and desire marriage." I never thought too much of that interaction until recently, but since that time I've had so many emotional ups and downs and fears that I would *never* get married—especially God's way. I was a hot, single mess. Looking back, even if I had met a marriage-minded man, he probably wouldn't have known what to do with me and perhaps would have just walked away. Yet, throughout those years after that encounter, I was blessed to hear the diverse testimonies of my sisters in Christ who married God's way. Those testimonies and some personal encounters with God quieted my spirit, gave me the courage to face and overcome my fears, and gave me an unshakeable faith that God can help me and *you* marry His way. It doesn't mean that I don't still have doubts. I have moments where I think, "How is this really going to happen?" But I think about the times God did more than I could have even thought to ask, and I fight to hold on to the faith in my heart that He does care about me and will move on my behalf concerning my desire for marriage. So the insights that I share are ones that I know can help you (as I like to say) "live right, love life, and find Mr. Right."

If you don't know my style by now, I'll tell you what it is so that you can get everything I want you to get out of this book. I like to break down the Word of God by providing step-by-step strategies and teaching points so that you can practically live it. I love the Word of God and I'm a witness that despite our shortcomings, past mistakes, and current sin, nothing is impossible once it's engrafted in your spirit and manifested in your natural life.

So in this chapter we're going to talk about things that *could* be keeping you single. Some of these are reasons why I was personally a hot, single mess. Just keep in mind that everyone is different and these things may or may not apply you. But these are things that could be keeping you in an extended single season when you could be married. Before we go any further, I want you to understand that I'm really challenging you to answer this question:

Are you ready to receive and capable of being what you're asking God for?

The term "Hot, Single Mess" has incited giggles and in some cases excitement to know more. But it's really no laughing matter. A "hot, single mess" is a woman whose efforts in the area of romance have left her worse off than when she started. She's probably single when she could have been married. Or her frustrations over a prolonged single season have led her to poor choices and desperation. I'm going to briefly cover some reasons that some of us stay single longer than necessary or why we never marry when we could have married. All of these reasons indicate that there is a general status in lack of readiness on your part for marriage. Now, I can't really know for sure that my extended single season or yours was part of God's plan for our lives. But again, I am in a place of ministering to women who are ready to tear down barriers that could be keeping them from marriage. Some of these or perhaps all of these reasons for singleness might not apply to you. But I do know that these things surely could have blocked Mr. Right out if I had met him before now. In fact, I could have met Mr. Right and driven him off! So just be open to considering if any of these reasons for extended singleness could be the culprit in your life.

You're Still Single Because...You're Waiting The Wrong Way

"But those who wait upon GOD get fresh strength.
They spread their wings and soar like eagles,
They run and don't get tired,
they walk and don't lag behind"

Isaiah 40:31, The MSG

"Wait on God for your husband, honey." If you're like me, you've heard that phrase more times than you care to admit. And because you've heard it so much, you're convinced that there's some secret code inside the phrase that will actually get you what you're waiting on—your Mr. Right! The only problem is you don't know what the secret code is, and you don't know how to get it from the people who keep blurting out that magical phrase! So you wait. But while you do, nothing happens; you grow more frustrated by the day and you start to wonder if God would mind if you just took matters into your own hands.

Before you do that, I'm here to tell you personally that waiting on God does not look like what happens when we literally wait around for something in our daily lives. **Waiting on God means that you are doing everything you can do to be ready to receive what you're asking God for.** Before I matured in my singles walk with God, I thought of waiting in the literal sense of the word. I thought of standing in a long line trying not to lose my patience. I thought of waiting in traffic for an hour or a few hours with nothing to do except listen to the radio or (if I properly planned) read. I even conjure up the image of waiting on a friend who is notorious for making the group late every time we go out! I want you to notice how in each scenario—in my mind—waiting went hand-in-hand with feeling annoyed. It was synonymous with frustration brewing just below the surface, and with wanting to get to the next stage already. I literally waited. No wonder I was so frustrated in my singles walk. All I knew was that I wanted to be somewhere else other than where I was, and I had no idea how to handle the fact that it didn't look like I was going to get to where I wanted to go anytime soon.

But with God, waiting is not like that.

Waiting on God means having the freedom to live your life and live it in a way that brings you closer to what you truly desire.

I believe that should be good news to today's single woman—especially the single Christian woman—who is wondering where Mr. Right is. If you go back to Isaiah 30:41, you'll notice that spread, soar, run and walk are *verbs*. This means you are active in your workplace, in your church, in your community, in your social circle, and in your relationship with God. You take action on the things you know God is calling you to do.

I think we often act from a place of desperation and confusion in the arena of love, relationships and desired marriage because we see waiting as just that—literally waiting for God to produce a husband while our whole life passes us by. But God has a plan for us and that plan touches on *all* parts of our lives, not just our marriages to our future husbands. It's a plan that will give us more joy than we can stand—even in hard, dark times—if we play our part and follow His lead all the days of our lives. God's plan might not match our timetable, and it might not produce a final result that we envisioned, but it will *always* be better than what we could ever dream up for ourselves. Ephesians 3:20 says the result is always exceedingly, abundantly above all that we can ever ask for or imagine. I don't know about you but when I really let that sink in, I stopped trying to plot and plan, and started following the Man with the master plan. I finally decided to wait in a way that would bring God glory and allow Him to fulfill the desires of my heart. I decided to get out of my own way and take the ultimate leap of faith. I decided that I was going to wait God's way.

So if you want to wait God's way, let's talk about what it really means and how to do it.

First, we need to know what we're waiting on. Part of the reason I struggled so much as a single woman was because I was so conflicted in my heart about marriage. Deep down inside I wanted to get married, but for several years I allowed external forces and even my own doubts to undermine that desire. At 17 I wanted to do it God's way. However, that desire was almost destroyed by my own doubts that God would really do that for me, listening to the negative reports of others, and my lack of a personal relationship with God. But God is faithful. He used my experiences in the military to draw me into an intimate relationship with Him. Since then, I developed my own personal relationship with Him, I see myself differently, and I acknowledged and embraced my desire for marriage. But the best thing I could have done was place that desire in His hands and allow Him to work on me and prepare me for a lasting marriage with the man He has for me. So decide right now. Do you want to be married? Do you want to date and marry God's way? And do you want a godly husband? If you answered yes to all three of these questions, let's keep going!

Second, waiting on God often requires a shift in your mindset and behavior. Let's start with your mindset. Most likely you need to shift your thinking from "What is God going to do for me?" to "What do I need to do to be ready to receive what I've asked God for?" This goes back to our concept of waiting. Waiting in God's way means that you are in an energy mode to receive what God has for you. That means you've done what's necessary to receive it and keep it—you didn't just put your life on hold and wait for

God to give it to you. Sometimes you'll also need to work on what you think about yourself, what you think about God, and what you think about men. For example, I've found that it's common for women to think, "Where am I going to find a man like the one I really want in today's culture?" or "Why would God do something like that for me?" or "I don't know why a man would value me enough to marry me according to God's standards."

If you've ever asked or said things like this to yourself, you'll need to address the root cause of these thoughts and beliefs. Then start saying "God loves me and desires His best for me," and "Good men are everywhere," and "I am worth the wait." Then once you believe it, you'll be primed to change your behavior. You'll most likely change your behavior in a way that supports what you believe. You'll start to interact differently with men who clearly do *not* seem to have the same values as you. You'll also act differently with men who *do* have the same values as you.

Third, waiting on God requires not fainting while you prepare and wait for His promise. I take this concept from the scripture Galatians 6:9, NLT, which says, "So let's not get tired of doing what is good. At just the right time we will reap a harvest of blessing if we don't give up." If you think of reaping and sowing in literal terms, that's hard work! If you've ever prepared, plowed, or worked in a field, you know it's hard physical work. Even gardening is almost like a workout. But the work is necessary to get the end result—a field or garden full of crops that were planted in the appropriate season.

Some people believe that you shouldn't work to find a mate. I agree that when you work, your intent shouldn't be to find a mate. But you should work to make an active, fulfilling, and rewarding life for yourself. As a single woman, you should have a life full of interests, hobbies, activities, and relationships in community, work that fulfills you, and love. Your desire for marriage would naturally fall into perspective in light of how you live your life, because you're living in a way that brings you closer to your desires. So many singles literally wait for a spouse to show up before they start to live out dreams like travelling abroad, buying a house, pursuing higher education, or just being a part of their local community. I can definitely understand that because when you're achieving your dreams, you say in your heart to God, "I sure wish I had someone to share this experience with." I remember thinking that at certain milestones in my own life. But the truth is that even as a single woman, if you have an active life, you stand a greater chance of having close friends and even family to share in those events with you. You'll also be in a better position to meet men you actually want to date. Don't fall into the trap of just going to work, church, and the gym. Don't become the workaholic who's married to her job. And don't be the single woman who's so wrapped up in the ministries at church that you can't make time for new people in your life. Get active, get involved in your local community, and get a life!

You're Still Single Because...You're Listening to The Wrong People

As a Christian who is trying to grow in the knowledge of God so that you can live a godly life, you must choose your friends wisely. Now, don't make the mistake of believing others aren't good enough to be your friend. That's not Christ-like. Jesus "befriended" people who were not friend material in order to accomplish God's mission: to show love to a dying world. So it is good be a friend to someone who just does not have God in his or her life. You never know how what you say or do—based off the love of God—will impact them, and you want to always keep the opportunity open to witness to someone so that their soul will be saved.

On the other hand, you cannot afford to let just anyone into your inner circle. Your inner circle influences your view of yourself, of God, and of the world. So if you allow others to come into your inner circle and you don't know who they are, what they believe and what their motives are, their influence could lead you further away from God. If you allow people into your inner circle after you have a clear understanding that they have no respect or fear for God, no regard for you or your life, or no set goals in life you are setting yourself up for failure. And as a single woman, the wrong inner circle can lead you to make mistakes with men that are hard to recover from. If you're already in your 30s you don't have the same amount of time available to you as you did in your teens and 20s to achieve your personal or God-given goals. Later on, we'll talk about who you want to accompany you on this journey and who needs to be loved from a distance.

If you need a support system and community of women who can be forthright about the struggles they've faced and can provide biblical strategies on dating to courtship, join me at authorofmyfaith.com/letstalkcommunity. It's the Let's Talk About It Community for single women who want a safe place to discuss their dating and relationship challenges. I lead and moderate each chat night and community call to ensure a safe environment and that all strategies taught are biblically sound and proven in yielding success in dating and courtship.

You're Still Single Because…You Haven't Healed From a Past/Recent Hurt or Trauma

During my Isaiah 30 encounter with God, it was almost like He was saying, "It's not me, it's you, Beloved. You are the reason you're still single." He didn't actually say those words, but looking back on the condition of my heart, mind, body and soul He would have been right if He had said that to me. I had some hurts that left me insecure and believing deep down in my heart that I wasn't good enough to receive the very thing I deeply desired.

So I want to ask you some questions. What have you experienced in your life that's left you wounded, angry or broken? And I'm not talking about minor offenses. I'm talking about a parent who left and never came back. Or maybe physically or sexually abused you for years, or repeatedly left you with someone who did. Were you raped? Constantly bullied by older children at school? Called names repeatedly? Maybe you never felt accepted by other family members or were constantly compared to another sibling who was clearly "the favorite." Maybe you were born out of wedlock or were never told who one of your parents is. I could keep going, but I think I've listed enough tragedies to give you an idea of the things that happen to us that leave us wounded and unable to carry on in the way God intended for us to in this life.

We'll have a chapter later that will walk you through how to talk about whatever harmful experiences you've had in your life and some next steps to take to heal. If you don't take the time to heal now, that pain could keep you single or significantly hinder the relationship with the man God has for you.

You're Still Single Because...You Have No Life

"A man's gift maketh room for him, and bringeth him before great men."

Proverbs 18:6, KJV

So I've mostly used the Message and NLT up to now. But I had to use KJV to get this point across. A ministry that I used to follow was Finding Morris with James Riley. Unfortunately he passed away early in 2013. But I will always remember his words of wisdom to single and single, Christian women. One thing that he said is that "Your gift is what brings you in front of great men, so if you want to meet the right man, get out, get a life and use your gifts to serve others for the glory of God." I had never thought to apply that scripture in that way, but I personally take that to heart.

Here's why. Eve was created as a gift to Adam. Ruth was discovered by Boaz because she was serving her widowed mother in law and being a gift to her. Rebekah was determined to be a good fit for Isaac because she willingly and generously served his servant at a well. Although marriages were typically arranged during that time, each woman was either created for a special purpose for a particular man or was found to be the best fit for a particular man because of the gifts she brought through acts of service. So again, get busy with getting a life, and use your gifts to serve those around you!

You're Still Single Because...You Don't Know Who You Are

"So God created human beings in his own image. In the image of God he created them; male and female he created them."

Genesis 1:27, NLT

"This means that anyone who belongs to Christ has become a new person. The old life is gone; a new life has begun"

2 Corinthians 5:17, NLT

Before you're anything else, you are a child of God who Jesus Christ died a brutal and gruesome death on a cross for so that you would have a right to the tree of life and a chance to have eternal life. Beyond that, though, I believe God has given you the will and capacity to discover the unique person He's designed and created you to be. What are your spiritual and natural gifts? What is your personality like? What character traits do you naturally have? What areas of temptation tempt you the most? These are just a few questions to help you scratch the surface of knowing who you are, not just what you can do.

We will discuss this further in a later chapter, but I want to leave this with you. I was watching TD Jakes Mind, Body and Soul one Sunday. He had a panel of single, successful professional women who struggled for one reason or another in relationships. None of them had ever been married. At the end of the show, he gave them each a present. They opened it up and held these princess mirrors up with this look on their faces like "This man has lost his mind"! I waited to see what wisdom he was going to give and sure enough, what he said helped me as well. He said that the mirror was for them to remember that the answer to their dilemma was already inside them. He said that the moment they figured out who they really are would be the moment their journey to "Mr. Right" would take a completely different turn.

He's so right. Once I started to discover who I really was – not just what I can do – my journey took a completely different turn. So later on, we'll talk about how to discover or even re-discover the woman God created you to be.

You're Still Single Because...You're Soul Tied to the Wrong Man

"There's more to sex than mere skin on skin. Sex is as much spiritual mystery as physical fact. As written in Scripture, "The two become one." Since we want to become spiritually one with the Master, we must not pursue the kind of sex that avoids commitment and intimacy, leaving us more lonely than ever—the kind of sex that can never "become one." There is a sense in which sexual sins are different from all others. In sexual sin we violate the sacredness of our own bodies, these bodies that were made for God-given and God-modeled love, for "becoming one" with another."

1 Corinthians 6: 16-18, MSG

This version of this passage helped me understand what ungodly soul ties are. Although sex isn't the only way to form an ungodly soul tie, it's often the most devastating for women. I believe it takes longer to break a soul tie that was formed from sexual intimacy after emotional intimacy, than one that formed from being emotionally attached to someone but you fought tooth and nail to abstain sexually. This scripture alludes to this mystery.

What is clear, though, is that sex ties you to another person. This passage also says that pursuing casual sex or sex without commitment leaves you in a worse condition. Since God's design for sex is only within marriage, even sex between two people who intend to marry and even "commit" to each other leaves them in a worse condition than if they were to abstain. It violates one of the purposes for our bodies, which is to become one with the right person in marriage. It also ties you to the wrong people.

If you don't break those ties, you will have unresolved issues if that relationship fell apart or you left on bad terms. In addition to that, all the memories, fantasies and spiritual attachments to the wrong people will negatively impact your ability to connect emotionally, spiritually, mentally and even physically to the right person. If you want to take the active step now to untie yourself from ungodly soul ties, here is an e-booklet that will get you started in that direction: http://goo.gl/oG5uxX.

You're Still Single Because...There's Something God Wants From You

"So if you sinful people know how to give good gifts to your children, how much more will your heavenly Father give good gifts to those who ask him."

Matthew 7:11, NLT

There seem to be a wide variety of opinions on God's will concerning marriage for our lives. Some people seem to believe in the gift of singleness, where people take the attitude of Paul and prefer to remain single. Some people believe that God withholds marriage from people who aren't ready. Others seem to imply that certain personality or character flaws prevent you from marrying or at least marrying well. These could be true. I believe that God has His own reasons for allowing each of us to marry when we do and that prolonged singleness can be due to God wanting to work something out in us during our single season. Lots of people who aren't ready or "qualified" for marriage are blessed by God to find someone to "have and to hold." So I take a slightly different attitude towards prolonged singleness. I believe in my heart of hearts that God wants us to marry and marry well, that we can get in our own way in regards to finding a suitable spouse, and that sometimes God wants to use our singleness for a particular or special purpose before we marry.

Maybe He wants to prepare you for the lifelong commitment that marriage is supposed to be. I've noticed that in general younger generations are marrying later in life. I'm not sure if it's cultural, as people who lived in the Bible days seemed to marry young and arrange their marriages. But I've often wondered if they were truly ready for what marriage was supposed to be as designed by God. Or, maybe He has a special assignment for you while you're still single. You were designed to be a helpmeet, so maybe He wants to teach you how to balance the duties of your calling before adding the responsibilities of a husband and children. Whatever it is, if He wants you to do something before you marry, waiting for marriage will be worth it.

Let's Pray

Now that we've talked about a few reasons for why you may be single, I want to pray with you. Part of my dream is to not only marry and marry well despite the odds, but to see a generation of young people (and even the no-so-young) who do the same. So if what you've been reading is speaking to your heart, don't give up. Acknowledge the desire and seek God for His final say on the matter. Here's a prayer to help you do that:

Lord Father God,

We thank you for sending Jesus as the all-sufficient sacrifice for our sins. We thank you for your love and for seeing us as worthy for Jesus to die on the cross. We ask you to forgive our sins both known and unknown.

And now we ask for you to reveal to us anything in us or in our lives that could be keeping us from marrying according to your will. Jesus came so we could have abundant life. You created Eve for Adam because you said yourself it was not good for him to be alone. Both male and female represent you in perfect union on the earth. So we ask that you reveal to us anything that is preventing this representation in our own lives if it's in your will for us to marry. We ask that you strip anything away from us that's not of you concerning this area of our lives. Ultimately, we ask that your will be done in and for our lives.

This we pray in your Son Jesus Name,

Amen

Chapter 3: What Are Your Motives for Wanting Marriage?

"People may be pure in their own eyes, but the LORD examines their motives"

Proverbs 16:2, NLT

God is. I love to write and still can't pick just one word in my vocabulary to describe Him. But I will say it's nothing short of amazing to me how He's used some of the most difficult situations in my life to break me, shake me, and mold me into the woman He always intended for me to be.

The situation that God used to expose my heart's motives for wanting marriage was when my father died October 2, 2012. Seven days before my birthday. Although the trauma and shock was painful to live through, his death did bless me because it brought me closer to God. I'll explain how.

I had flown home to Tampa for the funeral and stayed for two weeks total. After that, I had to return to my duty station at the time in Djibouti, Africa. I was managing to keep it together until my mother called and told me that my adopted "dad"—a man who (along with his wife) took me in like a daughter—had passed away. He was a Navy Chief and anyone who's served time in the Navy knows that a good Chief keeps your divisions and commands from falling apart. Well, I fell apart after we hung up. I stopped socializing. I lost my focus at work. I was irritable. My church attendance declined. I fell into biding my time and was ready to go home and move on with my life—whatever that was. I gave up and told God "You're going to have to show me in a new way that you really love me." I couldn't have gotten any lower unless you had buried me in the ground. For the first time, I surrendered control to God and waited to see what He would do.

One night while I was lying in my rack (my bed) I managed to pick up my Bible. It was marked for Isaiah 30. While I was reading it, I felt God speaking to me. If His voice were audible words and we'd had a conversation, it would have gone like this:

God: "Beloved, you've made marriage an idol."

Me: "God, you know that's not true. Despite everything I've been through, I have never worshipped another god besides you—at least not on purpose."

God: (sighing) "Beloved, you've made it an idol."

Me: (refusing) "God I know what your words says...Thou Shalt Not—"

God: "Then why do you keep questioning my ability to bless you in this area of your life? Why do you think marriage is the one thing I'm refusing to give you? Why aren't you focused on me? Why do you want to get married anyways?"

Me: (having no good response and dropping my head in complete shame) "Touché."

After that I put my Bible down and couldn't read it for about a month. That was hard to "hear." But just like Moses "turned" to investigate the burning bush, I eventually picked that passage up again because I knew I had to press further into this matter. What I found that night, though, was that I didn't even *realize* I had made marriage an idol! Remember how I said my father's death was also a blessing? Well, it made me realize how alone I felt during the grieving process. I felt alone because I was still single. I knew I had God and I did have a few people I could have reached out to, but my conversation to God went something like this "Why can't I have a husband to lean on during this time in my life? You gave HER a good husband and she's a bigger mess than I am!" Then I wondered if I would ever get married. It all went downhill from there, and all the progress I'd made on my single's walk in the past year was leveled back to ground zero.

I could give myself credit and say that I'd faced a difficult time in my life and that this was the reason I felt that way. But the truth is that hardships bring out what's already inside you—whether or not you knew those things were there. I thought God was being cruel, when in fact He was being merciful in showing me my heart's condition by exposing my motives for desiring marriage. I say He was merciful because He could have allowed me to keep that buried in my heart unchecked. The good news is that before that night was over, I also felt God saying that the minute I could tear down that idol was when I would be ready to marry His way. It was like He was a father saying, "You will have what you're asking for when you get yourself together, and not a moment before!" I also felt Him asking me why I wanted to be married. Looking back I realized He wanted me to have the right perspective about a husband and about marriage before marrying. He wanted me to understand that even if He blessed me with my heart's desire right then and there, He still wanted to be first.

It's a good thing that God met me at Isaiah 30 that night, or else that setback could have been permanent. He could have left me to wallow in my self-pity and continue to become the very woman that repelled a Mr. Right. But He didn't. Instead, ***He took me on a journey to true contentment and taught me some very valuable lessons about preparing for a godly husband***.

So... Why do you want to get married?

So many things are implicated by this question, and you'll miss the lesson if you don't really think through it. Do you know what a marriage is really about? Do you know the work that's involved in sustaining a marriage? Do you understand the reasons for divorce? Do you know what the Bible says are grounds for a divorce? What would you do if your husband did the unthinkable to you? Leave? Stay but hold a grudge? Or find a way to resolve, forgive, and move on? I believe God was asking me why I wanted to be married to help me see that I wanted to be married for all the wrong reasons. Therefore, if I had gotten married, what do you think would have happened to my marriage? Bingo! It most likely would have fallen apart. Now, I know for a fact that some couples do get married for the wrong reasons and are still able to work through the issues that come along with it. But think of all the unnecessary heartache they have to go through. They may even really love each other, but that love is eclipsed by the fact that most of the work they're doing in their marriage for a period of time is focused on salvaging their marriage, not building or strengthening it.

So to keep you from falling into that trap, I'm going to identify some of the wrong reasons single Christian women want to get married. Then I'll talk about the right reasons to want marriage.

1) I finally get to have sex. When you get married God's way, yes, you finally get to have sex. But let's stop and think about all the reasons couples stop having sex: stress, illness, family deaths, hardships, attraction to other people, and the list goes on. The bottom line is that once you get married, there will be stresses on your marriage that will make sex a low priority if you don't invest in or fight for your marriage. And if sex is a top reason for wanting marriage, then a lack of sex could break your marriage once you finally do marry.

2) All my other friends are married. I'm the last single woman standing. I know. It makes you wonder what's wrong with you that you're the last single one in the bunch. It's just like when you're the last one picked for the sports team at recess. But it's really not. When you're on God's team, timing is according to what He has planned for each individual. Meaning, just because someone gets married before you do doesn't mean automatically mean that something is wrong with you. It could mean that on God's terms it was time for them to get married and your time will come later.

3) It's time for me to settle down. Sarah thought it was time for her to have that baby God promised her and look at what happened. She created a painful and violent situation in her own home. Don't allow other people's ideas and notions—or your own, for that matter—to dictate when you believe you should get married. I know the biological clock is real. But so are God and His power. I know we aren't living in the Bible days, but God is alive and He still gifts us with miracles every day.

4) I'm tired of always doing important things by myself. I totally get it. But your marriage is more than having a date for company parties, church gatherings, and other events. You want someone there during the good times, but it means nothing if you have someone who isn't there when it really matters. Remember your vows say sickness and health. For richer or poorer. You want someone who will be there in the bad times, too.

5) I want someone to provide for me. Wanting security in and of itself is not wrong. But again, God is a god of priorities. He wants to be first. Even if you get married and become a stay at home wife, who do you think is giving your husband his source of income? God is. You still have to remember that God is your provider.

On the contrary, there are definitely right reasons to want to marry, and I believe God will honor those. Here are some of mine:

1) To produce godly children
2) To have a lifelong, covenant commitment in a godly union
3) To serve God better
4) To help someone live out their God-ordained purpose
5) To have someone help you live out your God-ordained purpose
6) To build a life with another believer
7) To be an example to others who would make great husbands and wives, but don't know how to do it God's way

I encourage you to discover what the right reasons would be for you. But I also encourage you to distinguish the difference between reasons and benefits. Notice how I said, "I finally get to have sex" is a wrong reason. But let's be honest...it's a *great* benefit! And God says so, too. He created the act and wants us to enjoy it, but to do so in the safe place of a marriage that He has ordained.

Now, going back to this idol that had formed in my heart...

I wondered why I felt that God had a sense of urgency when He let me know that I'd made marriage an idol. This scripture came to mind:

You must worship no other
gods, for the LORD, whose
very name is Jealous, is a
God who is jealous about
his relationship with you.

Exodus 34:14, NLT

In the context of my singles walk, this is what He revealed to me. ***Because I'd made marriage an idol, I left no room for God to work in that area of my life.*** Let's say God allowed me to have my heart's desire and marry my Mr. Right before I worked that issue out. I would have made my husband my god. The spirit of idol-worship doesn't leave just because you get what you wanted. It transfers to the object of your desire, and gives that object a greater influence and importance over your life than God. So instead of thanking God for what He's given you, you end up worshipping the actual person or thing He's given you.

In the context of my father's death, I want to share the main lesson at the heart of each thing I learned about my singles walk. When I got back to Djibouti, I felt out of place. It was business as usual, except it wasn't for me. I felt the urge to withdraw. I knew there were people I could reach out to for support, but looking back I realize that God had been trying for some time to get me all to Himself. My desire for a husband or a support system was the thing that God used to get me to realize that He alone was the orchestrator of my life. I'd lost focus of that without even realizing it.

God wanted me to come back to Him for restoration, guidance, love, and so that He alone could be the focal point of my life. This lesson is at the root of everything I will share with you in this book. As Exodus 34:14, NLT says, He's jealous over His relationship with you. He doesn't want you to worship idols because those idols have a destructive power over you. They can't offer you a relationship, life, or sustenance. They only destroy and devour your energy and free will. But God wants to fulfill His promise of hope and a future for your life. When you delight yourself in Him, He wants to fulfill the desires of your heart.

So if after reading this chapter, you feel that you've made marriage an idol, we'll talk later about how to put marriage and a husband into the proper perspectives. For now, I want you to take these steps to put God back in His rightful place as the No. 1 priority in your heart:

1) Repent. God is a god who disciplines, corrects, and provides consequences for our actions. But He is also a god who is merciful. He has a heart filled with compassion for our condition and is always thinking of ways to draw us back to Him (2 Samuel 14:14)! So tell Him you're sorry for putting another person in His place. But don't just say it. Mean it in your heart and resolve not to do it again.

2) Decide that you will keep God first. I'll be the first to admit that this is easier said than done. The cares of this world will often compete with God's place in your life. But let's keep them in perspective. If you're busy—even with good things in life—God is the one who allowed you to have something to busy yourself with. After all, God commanded mankind to "be fruitful and multiply." He wants us to be productive, but He also wants to be in first place. So I'll also be the first to admit that when I put God first, it's amazing how the things that I struggled so hard to make happen just seemed to fall into place with ease when I placed them into God's hands.

3) Find a way to hold yourself accountable. Something that works for me is to talk to someone I trust to keep my confidence. Close friends are good, but make sure this person is someone who won't repeat what you tell them. Even better, consider a pastor who is skilled in counseling, a certified counselor, or even a chaplain. I would also find a mentor who has been where you are and can explain the steps to get to where you want to go. I'm more than happy to assist you with that as well. You can contact me at afi@authoroffaithmin.com and ask questions about your particular situation.

4) Make a standing "date" with God. Some people say it's a hard and fast rule that you have to commune with God early in the morning. Although I have done it and I can attest to how much of a difference it made in my day, I'm not a morning person. So I would sometimes have "quiet time" with God in the evening before I went to bed. The church I attend now – New Life Providence – has "soaking prayer" time. It quiets you and allows you to invite God's presence into your stillness. Whatever works for you, be sure to do it consistently. Remember that God is a god of pursuit. One of the things that makes Him happiest is when you pursue Him by making time to allow Him to fill you with His presence.

It may take time to "change your heart." That's understandable. What matters most is that you desire the change and that even when your emotions don't want to cooperate, your will seeks to fall in line with God's will. Keep doing these things over and over, as often as you need to. God will honor your desire and your commitment. Here are some questions to get you started in applying this information to your individual situation.

Have you wanted marriage for the wrong reasons? If so, which reasons listed previously applied to you? Did any other reasons that weren't listed apply, and if so what were they?

_____

_____

_____

Meditate on this scripture:

"You must worship no other gods, for the LORD, whose very name is Jealous, is a God who is jealous about his relationship with you."

Have you placed your desire for marriage before your desire for a relationship with God? Why? Or why not?

_____

_____

_____

Based off the things you may have done that prove your desire for marriage was placed above or before God, why do you think God is jealous of His relationship with you?

_____

_____

_____

_____

Have you wanted marriage for the wrong reasons? For you, what would be the right reasons?

_____

_____

_____

Chapter 4: What Mrs. Proverbs 31 Can Teach Us About Being Ready For Marriage…

"She is clothed with strength and dignity, and she laughs without fear of the future."

Proverbs 31: 25, NLT

I used to think that the Proverbs 31 passage only applied to married Christian women. Once I started this journey to contentment as a single and readiness for marriage I saw how it applied to me as well.

One thing God revealed to me in my preparation is that the true measure of a woman is not in her response to the good things in her life—or the response to her life when everything goes right. I call good times the summer and spring seasons of life. So our true measure is not even determined by the fall season because even fall brings the promise of a harvest for those who plant and toil in the spring and summer. Rather, the true measure of God's women is in the way they live their lives in the winter seasons of their lives—the seasons where it's hard to see the beauty of where God has placed you.

I believe God wants us to be women who are equipped to deal with all seasons of life, like the woman in Proverbs 31. I know for sure that one lesson God has taught me—with great patience, might I add—is how to be content in every situation in my life. I believe the reason it was so hard for me to accept being content as a single was because I believed this season of singleness was undesirable while marriage was desirable. Meaning, I bought into the lie that it is better to be married rather than single. The truth is that it's a season of life that simply has to occur before you marry. Every married person was once single, and most of the ones I talk to wish they'd had more preparation prior to marriage.

As I write this part of the book, I'm winding down my deployment to Djibouti, Africa. The heat, beaming sun and lack of rain make it feel like one long summer season! But as

I think about where I'm going—Virginia—I remember what winter seasons are like. I love real winters with snow, probably because I never had any growing up in Florida. I love the way it makes nature seem so surreal and peaceful. I love breaking out my boots, heavy jeans, sweaters, scarves and wool coats. In fact, I'm READY for the winter of 2014 and those to come after because I have sweaters, boots, and scarves galore! When I think about people who complain because it's too cold, I laugh because I know I'm still going to have a ball going here and there all bundled up in my favorite warm clothes.

I told you that because I believe it's the same way with the Proverbs 31 woman. She laughs at the future because she's prepared. I used to think that she was prepared because she just had it all together. But God taught me that you will always be prepared if you place all your trust in Him and not only learn to hear His voice, but also to heed His directions. When you can hear God's voice and do your absolute best to follow His instructions, you can never go wrong—even if you're considered a failure in the world's eyes.

So let's examine the concept of readiness through the perspective of being single and desiring marriage. I don't think a person can ever truly be 100 percent prepared for marriage. But after meditating on the example of the Proverbs 31 woman, I believe there are some qualities that indicate that you are ready to marry God's way.

You know who you are and you have a personal relationship with God

"Charm is deceptive, and beauty does not last;
but a woman who fears the LORD will be greatly praised" Verse 30

It's amazing to me that anyone can go through life and not know who they really are. But we do. So we focus on what others say about us, and what our outer woman looks like more so than the person we are on the inside. But the Proverbs 31 woman was described with so many rich, inner qualities that make her sound like the woman you want to know!

Above all else, she is a woman who knows her identity in God through Jesus Christ. As a single woman, I believe we should seek to do this before we seek to marry well. To know our identity in Christ means we understand that although we are dearly beloved to God, we are sinners and were bought by the sacrifice of God's only begotten son, Jesus Christ. This was done to save our souls from eternal damnation after our physical death. Once that completely sunk in for me, I had a stronger commitment to follow and serve God— despite mistakes, temptations, frustrations, and even days I didn't feel like it.

And you can't truly marry God's way completely without having a personal relationship with God. Your relationship with God is the foundation of your life. If you don't have it, how can you have a godly marriage with another human being? To sum it up, Acts 17:28 says that God is the reason for our existence. Without Him, every relationship becomes that much harder to maintain and cultivate. But when you know who you are and your relationship with God puts Him first, you're well on your way to receiving what God has for you.

You are pursuing your life's purpose

Her hands are busy spinning thread, her fingers twisting fiber.

She extends a helping hand to the poor and opens her arms to the needy (Verses 19-20)

Although being busy just for the sake of having things to do is an enemy to establishing a relationship with God, God does honor when we "get busy" doing what He calls us to do for His namesake. Notice how Mrs. Proverbs 31 was busy doing things that prospered her business, her family and the agenda of God. And I'm willing to bet that this type of activity was honored because she was a wise woman who knew when and how to rest and fill herself back up so that she could continue to do what God called her to do.

Your life's purpose is worthy of pursuit. As long as you're not neglecting yourself, your friends, family, loved ones, or even your personal time with God, He will honor your efforts. He'll honor your pursuit of your purpose and even instruct you in the best way to pursue it.

You want to give first and receive second

I didn't put a scripture with this point because I would have had to put half the passage regarding Mrs. Proverbs. That's because her efforts were in *giving*. Notice how each activity she was involved in had some end of benefiting someone else. Then, in return she received praise from her husband, children, and others in her community.

But now, let's still put this concept of putting others first into perspective. I remember what James Riley – founder of Finding Morris, a Christian singles ministry – said about giving in marriage. He said that marriage is the big give. He explained that so often, we jump into marriages thinking that our spouses are going to give to us first. In reality, though, both spouses are called to give to each other selflessly. In order to do that, there's an order of putting others first that goes like this: God first, your self-care second, your spouse third, and everyone and everything else comes after. In order to truly care for your spouse in the way he'll need you to, God will have to fill you with His love first. You'll also need to take care of your individual physical needs so that you have enough to give your spouse. So often I think we believe that our own desires and preferences are supposed to come first in a marriage, so some of us choose spouses who will accommodate that or resent spouses who expect us to accommodate that. But the truth is that we're called to put our spouses first, and we do that by making sure that we care for ourselves first so that we have that overflow to give them.

And so it was with Mrs. Proverbs 31. She gave and gave because she was overflowing with the goodness that God placed in her. I'm sure that came from being able to put God first and making sure that she attended to her own needs, so that she could give in abundance to those in her life. And in return she received an outpouring of appreciation, adoration, and love.

You are patient and accepting without tolerating things that disrupt a godly home.

Mrs. Proverbs 31 did *not* sleep on her watch! Another term we use in the military is "Not on my watch", which means that unacceptable, criminal or substandard behavior will not be tolerated under my leadership. This is the spirit I felt while meditating on the passage about Mrs. Proverbs 31. The Message version of this passage explains that she kept active watch over every *body* in her home. She was not going to answer for God for sinful activity that she could have prevented her loved ones from indulging in. She understood the serious responsibility she had as the keeper and instructor of the souls under her roof.

I learned this through work. I have learned how to be a manger that accepts people for who they are, but doesn't tolerate a violation of standards. When you tolerate a violation of standards that are meant to ensure the success of your operation, everyone goes down. And as a leader, if you didn't know about it that's just more ammunition to relieve *you* from your position!

Likewise, in your home, when you tolerate an ongoing violation of God's standards (which are meant to keep you safe), you invite all kinds of evil into your home. Yet, there's power in accepting a person for who they are—strengths, weaknesses, and all. When you do this, you take away the defenses people put up when they believe you only want to expose their weaknesses for your personal gain. You also empower that person when you assign them tasks according to their abilities and strengths. When their defenses are down and they feel empowered, they're primed to receive the correction and instruction that God intended for you to provide.

So practice this now with your family, friends, and those who report to you at work. Don't tolerate the violation of much-needed standards, and keep everyone—including you—above board.

You can let go of a grudge even though you are truly upset.

> When she speaks, her words are wise,
> and she gives instructions with kindness. (Verse 26)

This is important. Now, notice I didn't say you never get upset or you never address wrongdoing. Even the Bible doesn't command you to never get angry—it only instructs us not to sin in our anger. And I understand why, because it's often when we're angry that we speak in an ill manner to others and say things we can't take back. It's not often that people are drawn to or even tolerate someone who doesn't know how to talk to people. And if they do, it's often because that person has something they need.

But Mrs. Proverbs 31 knew how to talk to people. If she didn't, her husband and children probably wouldn't praise her like they did. Later on in the passage, she's described as *always* having something kind to say to someone who needed encouragement. That's no easy feat. People get on our nerves; say things out of turn, and step on our toes. But if we allow the annoyance and offense to rot in our spirits, we'll find ourselves speaking and acting the same way in return.

So let's follow the examples of Mrs. Proverbs 31, and turn to God to help us learn how to face and overcome offenses so that we can fill God's desire for us to be good and speak well to those He places in our care.

You can submit to a husband's leadership without losing yourself.

> Her children stand and bless her. Her husband praises her:
> "There are many virtuous and capable women in the world,
> but you surpass them all!" (Verses 28-29)

In another verse, Mr. Proverbs 31 is described as a man who is well known at the "city gates." I took this to mean a number of good things. Maybe he's a well-known and respected businessman or leader in their city. Maybe he's a strong leader in their church. Whatever he did, he did it well and it commanded the respect of his community. However, he still praises his wife for who she is and all that she adds to his life. Why? She's probably a key element to his success with his peers and those he interacts with on a daily basis. Not only is she a good wife because she's good to him, but she's a good mother and she's capable and professionally renowned in her own right. Who wouldn't take notice of that and think well of him?

But there's always the question of who's the leader in the home. I believe that God designed Adam to be the head of the family unit. Adam was created first and given a task. But then God decided that it wasn't good for Adam to be alone, so He created Eve to be his helper. So then the question is for what task was Eve created to help Adam? To be fruitful and multiply. God created Eve under His care and as a vital element to Adam's success in carrying out his assigned task, as Adam was submitted to God's authority.

When someone is assigned to you as a helper, that means you create the vision and plan while they fill a critical role in helping you make sure that the vision or plan is carried out. But the beauty of this arrangement for Adam and Eve is that God designed the woman to be influential and in a sense equal to her husband. How do I know? Because she was taken from his rib—his side. If your rib cage collapses, you're done! Likewise, when a man's "rib" (his wife) suffers, the whole house suffers as well.

Also, take into the account again the Proverbs 31 woman and the role of Deborah, the judge. Each woman was greatly loved and lauded as a wonderful wife by her husband, but each had great influence on her husband. So their husbands didn't feel threatened by their success or strength, but rather encouraged it while still maintaining their position as the head of the household. And this is what God wants for you when you marry. He wants you to submit to your husband's authority as you flourish professionally and personally.

Chapter 5: Fundamental Truths about Sex, Love, Dating and Romance

Now it's time to get to the foundation of your belief systems. This is what you'll build your personal and lifestyle transformation on. Since you picked up this book, you're probably struggling with any combination of these things: self-esteem issues, the consequences of poor relationship choices, lack of dating know-how, and frustration over the type of men you keep meeting. The good news is that you don't have to stay where you are. But you won't be able to rebuild yourself or your lifestyle until you uncover your current belief system and change it. So as it pertains to dating, courtship, and marriage, we have to talk about the truth—God's truth—when it comes to sex, love dating, and romance.

I used to think the Bible was silent on all these things. But then I read Song of Songs and other accounts of men and women in the Bible going through what we call the dating process. Although dating is something we do now and things like casual sex are culturally acceptable in America, the romantic exchange between the two lovers in Song of Songs is enough to make a grown man blush! So after reading this book, I started meditating on specific scriptures and passages in the Bible to find out what else God had to say about what really goes on between a man and a woman that He placed together with the purpose of marriage. What I found was more than enough to reset my beliefs about sex, love, dating, romance, and marriage.

What I'm offering is my individual experience with God and His Word. So if it inspires you to tweak it to fit your unique situation, that's okay. I just want you to rebuild your belief system and lifestyle around biblical principles.

The Truth About Sex Outside of Marriage

To be clear, sex outside of marriage is a sin in God's eyes. It's sexual immorality as anything but sex between a man and a woman joined in marriage is sin (Hebrews 13:4, 1, Corinthians 7:2, Galatians 5:19-21). I know I'm just as susceptible to falling into this sin as we all are, but I'm committed to abstinence from sex outside of marriage. I never push my stance on sex outside of marriage on others—which is that I strive to follow God's standard and abstain from sex outside of marriage. I don't push it for three reasons. First of all, I understand what it's like to fall into sexual temptation because you don't know any better or because you were never convicted of God's standard for this area of your life. Second, I don't want to make anyone feel condemned for not agreeing or for making that mistake. Third, it is not for the faint of heart. It requires a lifestyle overhaul in many cases that men and women just don't want to go through. They'll say it's unattainable when the truth is that it isn't. You just have to be brave enough to make the decision to live a lifestyle that will actually support it.

If that's how you feel reading this—that abstaining from sex outside of marriage is unattainable—I want to ask you a question I once heard Michelle McKinney Hammond—an author who champions for single, Christian women—ask . A young woman was pouring out her heart about how it was so hard to abstain from sex outside of marriage. She was frustrated and upset that her friends and the men she dated kept challenging her to let that silly standard go. Michelle was chomping at the bit to answer her! Her response to the young woman was something along these lines: "Well, how has having sex outside of marriage worked for you so far? You're still single and you've never been married." So I'll ask you...how has having sex outside of marriage worked out for you? How many men do you regret having sex with? Please don't feel that I'm implying that you're bad or wrong, because I've asked myself these questions, too. I just want to frame this issue in a way that allows you to see the truth—God's truth—about having sex outside of marriage.

Another moment of clarity came not too long ago. I met a young minister at a conference. We went out for lunch and he made it quite clear that he was physically attracted to me. Not many of his questions were geared towards getting to know me as a person. Instead, they were designed to help him figure out whether or not I fit the expectation of what he felt he deserved in a woman. The most shocking part of our conversation went something like this:

Minister: "How much time do you need before having sex?"

Me: (after thinking "This dude has *got* to be kidding me...") "What do you mean? I'm not having sex outside of marriage."

Minister: "So then what happens when you're married and have sex and realize you're not compatible? Are you just doomed? I mean, it's kind of like test-driving a car, right?"

Me: "So what you're saying is that women are objects to you and you feel you need to test drive them to see if they're suitable to your sexual demands. And no...it's *not* like test-driving a car. I'm a woman, not an object—not a car."

Before you think I'm harsh, let me explain what else went on in that conversation prior to this point. He talked about how he didn't want someone who had been sexually abused, yet he wanted a freak in the bedroom. He also hinted that he needed a woman who fit the image of the first lady— he was a pastor, after all! None of his "requirements" had anything to do with who the woman was as a person: her heart, character, mind, or spirit. They all were tied to sexual performance and being able to keep up appearances. I got the impression that he believed that sex was something to be used primarily for his benefit. It was obvious that he was not in agreement with God about reserving it for marriage. And he's a minister.

Why did I share this with you? To show you: 1) what lots of men really think of women they try to have sex with, 2) why having sex outside of a God-ordained marriage is not God's best for you, and 3) what having sex outside of marriage actually does to you. I also used both these situations to help explain clues to look for in your conversations and interactions with men to help you see when a man isn't honoring you, nor has any desire to abstain from sex outside of marriage.

What men really think of women they try to have sex with

First, let me explain what I mean when I say, "What men really think of women they try to have sex with." I'm talking about when a man tries to have sex with you prior to any type of real relationship. When this happens, a man generally sees you as a means to an end. It often looks like this: You've gone on a few dates, he paid for dinner or a gift, and now he's making sexual advances towards you because he wants to have sex with you. If you never told him that's what you wanted and find yourself in that situation, either you missed the red flags or you may not have clearly communicated (verbally or physically) that you didn't want to have sex with him. Either way, he's out for one thing only: sex. He doesn't really care about you as a person. He may or may not be interested in seeing you again after you have sex.

Men who try to have sex with you without any type of commitment see you as an object to use. If they like you after they've given you your test drive, they'll try to keep you around for long-term use. If they don't, they simply disappear. And if you are reading this book, I know you want the exact opposite. You want a man who will obey God's standards just like you want to obey them. You want a man who not only wants a wife, but a man who wants to make you his wife. Later on in the book, I'll cover how to avoid these types of men.

Why sex outside of marriage is not God's best for you

1) It creates ungodly soul ties.

> And don't you realize that if a man joins himself to
> a prostitute, he becomes one body with her? For the
> Scriptures say, "The two are united into
> one."[d] 17 But the person who is joined to the Lord is
> one spirit with him. 18 Run from sexual sin! No
> other sin so clearly affects the body as this one
> does. For sexual immorality is a sin against your
> own body.
>
> 1 Corinthians 6:16-18, NLT

This scripture says to run from sexual sin because no other sin affects your body like this one. You're tying yourself to another person, which means you become connected to them in a way that affects not only your body, but your spirit, too. Soul ties are beautiful when they are God-ordained. Ungodly soul ties keep you tied to the wrong man, which means you won't be able to accept the right one when he comes along.

2) It hinders the process of learning who a person truly is.

"Love covers a multitude of sins." This is something James Riley (may he rest in peace) of *Finding Morris* used to say. He explained that when you're in love with a person and you are having sex with them, you will explain away any red flags you see. That makes sense. How many times have you ignored minor or major red flags because you fell in love with a man and made him your lover?

In your new lifestyle, just remember that having sex outside of marriage makes you more susceptible to ignoring signs that would show you the man you desire just isn't right for you.

3) It feeds an appetite that was never meant to be created.

I believe that when you're having sex outside of the way God intended, it creates an appetite that is hard to control. That scripture says that no other sin affects the body like sexual sin. I suspect that it's because that person's spirit becomes joined to yours. All their sin, filth, and secret struggles become attached to you—and yours become attached to them. I believe that's probably why God only wants you joined to someone who He's ordained for you.

Let's take a quick look at King David. Although David was a king, he was living outside of God's original design for marriage—one man and one woman. He had several wives and concubines. Although that was culturally acceptable at the time, I think that practice helped open the door to other perversions and unnatural practices. But back to David. Despite his exploits for God, he's most known for his affair with Bathsheba and how he killed her husband to cover up her pregnancy after their first sexual encounter. I used to wonder how David—a great and mighty man of God—fell into such a tremendous sin. What came to me is that his conscience had already been eroded. Look at how many wives and concubines he had! If you read the account of his rise to the throne in the books of Samuel in the Bible, you'll see that he was never denied any woman he wanted. He, like many men in his culture, was already living in sin by having sex with multiple women. That practice must have led to an appetite and urge to have more women whenever he desired. Unfortunately for David, he didn't stop himself once he found out that Bathsheba was married.

Likewise for you, when you have sex outside of God's design for marriage, you open yourself up to fall further and further away from His design. Perversions and unnatural practices might eventually cease to shame you or cause you to pause and you'll fall further and deeper into behaviors and lifestyles that God just doesn't want for you.

Avoiding Sexual Temptation and Overcoming Loneliness

Two people are better off than one, for they can help each other succeed. If one person falls, the other can reach out and help. But someone who falls alone is in real trouble.

Ecclesiastes 4:9-10, NLT

In order to truly commit to a life of abstinence from sex outside of marriage, I've found that you have to master two things: avoiding sexual temptation and effectively dealing with loneliness.

First, let's talk about overcoming loneliness, because leaving it unchecked usually only feeds your likelihood to fall into sexual temptation. I've found that if you make it a point to meet new people and consistently build and strengthen true friendships, loneliness is not necessarily a bad thing.

Sure, you will have seasons where no matter what you do or how hard you try, you will not be on the same page as the friends and family members you are closest to. You won't see them for weeks or months; you won't talk to them very often; and the new people you're meeting just won't seem to want to build a deeper connection with you. We all go through that. But loneliness can actually signal that your budding relationships are not deep enough or you've been neglecting the good relationships that you do have.

Let's focus on a key phrase from Ecclesiastes 4:10:

...Someone who falls alone is in real trouble

As an introvert, it's not my natural tendency to hang out with large groups of people for extended periods of time. I love people and I work hard now to maintain the friendships and associations I do have, but large groups at a long period of time actually drain my energy. Extroverts can't understand because they don't know what to do with themselves if they can't be around people! But I understand that not having anyone to call on when I really need someone spells trouble. Likewise, I understand that I have to be there for others when they really need me—not just when I feel like it.

So in turn, I want to share with you how I used and am using my season of singleness to strengthen my relationships to guard against loneliness.

1) Reach out. Sometimes our relationships die out because we wait on others to always make the first move. Even though I'm an introvert, I will put myself out there and invite others to join me for movies, golfing, shopping, dining...anything fun. And I try to make as many invitations for outings as I can. This lets people know that you care about building and maintaining a relationship with them.

2) Make time for your relationships. Reaching out does no good if you don't have time to spend with the people you're reaching out to. Take a look at the activities you spend your time on and figure out whether they're really more important than spending time to build healthy relationships. I know some things have to be done in order for you to keep your commitments with your job or other activities. And if you're a single parent, your children should definitely be your priority. But if you have absolutely no time to spend building and maintaining your relationships with friends and family, you'll eventually find yourself alone in trouble when you really need them. And you'll be MIA when they really need you.

3) Be consistent. There will be times when you can't talk or visit as often. But do your best not to completely fall off your friends' and family's radar. I've been guilty of this. And every time I corrected myself, I found that I missed out and could have had deeper relationships with my friends and family if I had called or visited more often.

Now let's talk about avoiding sexual sin.

Let's go back to the definition of sexual sin: any sexual encounter or activity outside of marriage. To make it plain, that would include masturbation, sexual intercourse with men outside of marriage, homosexuality, sexual assault, and pedophilia. And get this—just imagining the act is a sin! Matthew 5:8 (NLT) say, "But I say, anyone who even looks at a woman with lust has already committed adultery with her in her heart." So that means watching pornography would be a sexual sin as well.

I'm giving you a definition so you can fully embrace the strategies to overcome it. It's hard to overcome something if you don't have a clear vision of what it is. So now that you have the definition, you simply have to stop participating in whatever sin you're engaged in. If you feel that you can't, you may need professional help from a counselor or even a pastor. But the first step is to stop, or at least make the decision that you are going to stop.

I know the arguments that homosexuality and masturbation aren't wrong. First, the Bible clearly states in multiple scriptures that homosexuality—just like having heterosexual sex with someone you are not married to—is outside the will of God. While I've never found any scriptures that talk about masturbation, I still want to pose a few things to you. One of my favorite authors, Michelle McKinney Hammond, made a point that has stuck with me for years, which is that masturbation makes it harder for your husband to learn how to please you. You learn how to satisfy yourself, so by the time he comes along you don't focus on how to communicate your desires, needs, and preferences. You've already figured out how to satisfy yourself.

Another problem you face with masturbation is that it's addictive. It's addictive because you form the habit of pleasing yourself whenever your body desires. Basically, you become ruled by your body. Although scriptures don't explicitly say, "Don't masturbate," they do tell us this: "You say, 'I am allowed to do anything'—but not everything is good for you. And even though 'I am allowed to do anything,' I must not become a slave to anything" (1 Corinthians 6:12, NLT). And that's exactly what masturbation does. It helps us become a slave to our sexual desires.

Once you decide to stop engaging in sexual sin, here are some ways to change your life to support the avoidance of sexual sin and mastery of sexual temptation.

1) Clean up your thought life. I believe Matthew 5:8 is also communicating the concept that the physical act of sex begins in our minds. It's impossible to completely break a soul tie to an old lover when you're constantly or periodically fantasizing about and longing for them. It's also difficult to avoid falling into sexual sin with a new man when you're constantly wondering if you are sexually compatible. So the first thing you'll need to do is get rid of any fantasies and sexual thoughts about any man who is not your husband. The thoughts will come. But that doesn't mean you need to let them play over and over in your mind. When they come up, change the visuals and thoughts in your mind. Focus on something else until the thoughts don't come up. Do that as many times as you need to in order to change your thoughts towards old lovers.

2) Change your atmosphere. I've found two things that will change your atmosphere quickly and supernaturally: anointing your living and work spaces with oil, and playing praise and worship music. I anointed my workspace with oil once and every problem that was there when I arrived was completely turned around! I also anointed my home before I moved in and now it's a place of peace where I often feel God's presence. I played some praise and worship one day late in the morning. As loud as it was, I fell asleep, into one of the best and most peaceful slumbers I've had in a long time. I believe it was because that music changed the atmosphere. I was reading the story about Willie Myrick who was kidnapped and held hostage for hours. While he was riding around with the kidnapper he said "Every Praise" by Hezekiah Walker. Eventually the kidnapper put him out! After that I read a blog article on his story that talked about how our worship and praise changes the atmosphere. Likewise in my church, I often feel God's presence strongly while we are in praise and worship. So much so that I have to weep—it's that overwhelming. So the next time you feel overwhelmed with sexual thoughts and urges, anoint your living space and engage in praise and worship. I think you'll find that it's hard to keep thinking about sex, an old lover, or even that new man you just met when you're truly trying to focus on worshipping God.

3) Guard your eyes. Romans 14:13 (NLT) says, "So let's stop condemning each other. Decide instead to live in such a way that you will not cause another believer to stumble and fall." This was stated in a passage that talked about how each believer in God and follower of Christ felt convicted to hold different standards they believed pleased God. In that same spirit, be mindful that what doesn't affect someone else may affect you. I believe that pornography or any variation of it will affect all of us. However, television shows with romantic undertones that are not pornographic may affect you while they may not affect your friend. Similarly, looking at an attractive man without certain articles of clothing for a long time (like longer than a few moments!) may cause you to think sexual thoughts before long. Another woman may not have that problem. So figure out what things negatively affect you when you look at them, and then avoid them. This is called protecting your eye gate.

4) Guard your ears. This is called protecting your ear gate. Romans 14:13 applies here as well. Know what you can and cannot listen to. If you know romantic or sexually charged songs leave you reminiscing on an old romantic relationship or wishing you just had the right man, don't listen to them. Be careful of the talk shows you listen to as well. I'll use myself as an example. When I was in my teens and early twenties, I liked R&B and some Hip-Hop music. Between the two genres, either I was listening to a woman swoon over some man she loved so much she could die, or I was listening to lyrics about parties and explicit and graphic descriptions of sexual encounters. No wonder I was depressed and battling images of sexual acts in my mind. Now, I pretty much only listen to a local Christian station: Victory FM 107.3 stationed out of Liberty University. The programmers have a mix of talk and music that is only biblically-based. I even went so far as to find the live stream on my TuneIn app and I play it sometimes at work and at home on my smartphone. This keeps me thinking about things that matter to God, like family, being financially responsible, and how to practically live out His Word in my life.

5) Stop communicating with and seeing ex-lovers and men who are only interested in sex. Do I think you can be friends with an ex-lover? Perhaps. Can you maintain a friendship with a man who only wants to have sex with you? Anything is possible. But for now, we need to focus on changing your thoughts and behaviors so you can break any ungodly soul ties and avoid falling into sexual temptation with new men. So cut all communication with ex-lovers until you completely break any soul ties with them. That means you should not call or text message him, receive his calls or text messages, or meet him anywhere (including each other's houses). For new men you meet who are only interested in sex, don't pursue anything further—not even friendship.

Friends spend time with people because they love them, not because they want to use them for their own benefit.

6) Find prayer and accountability partners. For women who were previously sexually active and enjoyed the sexual relationships they had with ex-lovers, completely breaking soul ties alone is an uphill battle. Even if you've managed to maintain your virginity, abstaining from sex when you're attracted to someone is a difficult feat. You'll need a prayer partner or accountability partner. Here is where knowing a person's character and capacity to keep your confidences are critical. This isn't something you need other people repeating unless you're comfortable with it being repeated. I believe there are many churches with loving members who want to help, but they're prone to gossip nonetheless. The point, though, is that breaking soul ties is something that's very difficult to do on your own. If you have a prayer warrior friend whom you know keeps your confidences, ask her to pray for your deliverance. If you have a pastor who's a good counselor, talk to him or her about it and ask them for prayer concerning your deliverance. Even better, confide in a competent counselor who can pray with you and help you devise healthy strategies to overcome the habits that support a lifestyle of sexual sin.

7) Be mindful of where you put yourself. Don't put yourself in situations where sexual sin is practically guaranteed. For instance, don't go on dates where you wind up alone with a man you're attracted to and who's attracted to you. Eventually, one of you is going to give in and things will go further than you intended—even if you don't complete the full physical act of sex. If you find that you missed the signals to avoid certain situations, get out of them as quickly as you can once you realize what's happened. Make an excuse if you have to. But get out of that situation before you pay more than you intended to pay or go further than you intended to go.

On Romance...

"Your left arm would be under my head, and your right arm would embrace me."

Song of Songs 8:3, NLT

That's right...the Bible describes a lover's embrace. Between husband and wife, of course! I chose that scripture to help you see that the Bible has plenty to say about romance, and that even the Bible describes the physical and sensual aspects of romance. The entire book of Song of Songs is about the passionate, juicy, and romantic exchange between a man and a woman. Some Bible scholars say the book was written by King Solomon, while others say it's simply an account of Christ's passion for his bride—the church. But honey, once you start reading that book, you won't deny that it's an obvious account of romantic love.

Our culture depicts romance as something that's done leading up to and throughout a sexual relationship. If you think about it, most romantic scenes in movies and books revolve around a man wooing a woman he desires sexually, with the end goal being sex. But the Song of Songs type of romance goes much deeper. The young man and woman explore the very being of the other. They enjoy the physical aspects of each other, but more than that they take into account their spiritual qualities. ***So, a Song of Solomon romance—which would lead up to a godly marriage through courtship—will have these qualities:***

1) It's a safe place. In Song of Songs 1:6, the young woman says to her lover, "Don't stare at me because I am dark—the sun has darkened my skin." She explains that it happened because she was forced to endure hard labor in the sun. Her confession reminds me of how we often feel insecure about our physical attributes, personal traits, and things that have happened to us in our past. But in her romance with her lover, she talks to him about it. His response is one of adoration. It's almost like she never even told him what happened to her. Likewise, you'll sense that the man for you will create a safe place where you can share past hurts and still be accepted.

2) Your purity will be valued. If you're still a virgin, your guy will value your purity in a Song of Songs romance. I've experienced the hatred, disgust, or misunderstanding that our culture has towards purity or even those who don't engage in promiscuity or common sexual practices. So the wrong men won't care about your virginity or your recommitment to God (if you're no longer a virgin). They'll only want to "romance" you for the end goal of sex and convenient companionship. But in this type of romance, your guy will cherish your purity because He understands the value that God says it has, and because his end goal will be marriage. Even if you are not a virgin—if you've recommitted your sexuality to God, he will honor that. He'll value your purity and if he hasn't adopted the same lifestyle yet, he will make the decision to respect God's standards and wait for you.

3) You'll be the only one. In Song of Solomon 2:16, the young woman says, "My lover is mine, and I am his. He browses among the lilies." In a verse in a previous chapter, she describes him as a man who many other young women notice and desire. Yet, as you read on, it's clear he only has eyes for her. Sure, he might have noticed other young women. But it's clear who his choice was—Miss Dark and Lovely!

I can't explain it because I haven't personally experienced it, but God has blessed me with enough examples to know that God-given attraction is what will drive faithfulness. Attention, time and romance are what feeds it and helps it flourish. When a man is able to see you with the eyes God has for you, he will see all the things that make it easy for him to be faithful to you, because God has changed you into a woman who is designed for a faithful man. Since you won't waste your time with a man who only wants to have you as one of many, the right man will see how different you are. He'll see your godly qualities, and the choice to be faithful to you—even in a sea of beautiful women who would go out of their way to please him—will be an easy one to make.

True Love...

"This is how much God loved the world: He gave his Son, his one and only Son. And this is why: so that no one need be destroyed; by believing in him, anyone can have a whole and lasting life."
John 3:16, MSG

While I was stationed in Djibouti, Africa, I struggled with the fact that God loved me. I mean, I knew He did. But it's one thing to know someone loves you and something altogether different to experience it. He had His ways—very small, but touching ways—of letting me know He loved me during that season of my life. But one night while I was in church, the experience of His love flooded me. I wept once I realized for the first time in my life how much He really loved me.

That came shortly after a "conversation" I had with Him while I was walking from my office to my living quarters. The chapel on the camp I was stationed at in Djibouti decided to show "The Passion" on a large screen. I decided to stop in even though I had already missed more than half of the movie. I came in right before the beating. I'd already seen the movie before so I wasn't sure why I felt compelled to see it again. Well, when the beating started I had to close my eyes. I refused to get up and walk out this time (the first time I got up and left until I felt like I could go back in). I figured if Christ could endure that, the least I could do was sit through the movie even if I couldn't watch. Of course I saw bits and pieces when I opened my eyes for a moment, but just hearing it tore me up. With tears streaming down my face, I asked God in my heart, "Why? Why would you let Jesus do this?" He asked, "Do you love me?" I said, "Of course I do." He said, "Will you do what I want you to?" I said, "Lord, after seeing and hearing that I'll do whatever you want me to do and go wherever you want me to go." What He said next floored me. He said, "Then it doesn't matter. It doesn't matter how bad it was." Tears ran down my face and I had to bury my face in my hands to keep from sobbing.

Now, fast-forward to me weeping in worship that night in church. I wept because I had flashbacks of Christ's beating and crucifixion. I remembered God telling me that

Christ's death was worth it if I gave my life to Him. I wept because I knew that even if I didn't commit to God, He would still love me. Still pursue me. Still have burning flames of love in His eyes for me. I wept because I knew He truly loved me, and that because of His love for me I was not condemned to a life in eternal hell—which I deserved—and I just could not conceive any word to express my gratitude.

After that experience, I came to understand that a husband will not love you as perfectly or completely as God does. A husband will fail you and hurt you. But ultimately, he will love you "as Christ loved the Church."

"Husbands, go all out in your love for your wives, exactly as Christ did for the church—a love marked by giving, not getting. Christ's love makes the church whole. His words evoke her beauty. Everything he does and says is designed to bring the best out of her, dressing her in dazzling white silk, radiant with holiness. And that is how husbands ought to love their wives. They're really doing themselves a favor—since they're already "one" in marriage."
Ephesians 5:25-30, MSG

I asked what that meant and what I received was this thought: Your husband won't do everything the way you like or when you want it. But he will commit to you. He will commit to your marriage. He will commit to raising your children. He will love you like he loves himself because you are a part of him.

This is what God taught me about true love between a husband and wife during my journey to being a former hot, single mess:

1) It bears all things. 1 Corinthians 13: 4-7. What happens when you do manage to get married and have some children and you don't lose that baby weight as fast as you thought you would? Or one of your children is born with a condition you didn't count on them having? Maybe you or your husband becomes ill or loses a job. Your parents or in-laws get sick or die. Whatever it is, true love between a man and a woman joined in marriage is strong enough to bear the weight of life's challenges, curve balls, and tragedies. And that's because God is in the middle of their love and their union.

2) It gives. It's "a love marked by giving, not getting." One thing I've noticed in how men and women relate to each other today is that men are quite accustomed to women pursuing them. To me, that means that if marriage ever happens after the dating process, the woman will always be the one giving up more than she planned to in order to get confirmation that her husband ever really loved her in the first place. In God's design, though, men who are dating a woman God's way will give their time, attention, and pursuit. And once they become husbands, God wants them to give their lives to their wives by committing, by being faithful and regarding them just as they would regard themselves. And as a wife, you're called to give as well.

3) It's meant to last a lifetime. God gave Adam his life's calling—to be fruitful and multiply. Then He created Eve and sent her to Adam to help him fulfill that lifelong calling. I believe that God's design for marriage was for it to be a lifelong commitment. I think divorce is such a disappointment to God because He gave us the ability and the make up to live in a lifelong relationship with one other person in marriage.

> "Didn't the LORD make you one with your wife? In body and spirit you are his. And what does he want? Godly children from your union. So guard your heart; remain loyal to the wife of your youth. "For I hate divorce!" says the LORD, the God of Israel. "To divorce your wife is to overwhelm her with cruelty,[d]" says the LORD of Heaven's Armies. "So guard your heart; do not be unfaithful to your wife."
>
> Malachi 2:15-16

God wants you to stay together, not divorce. And look what else He says. Ultimately He wants godly children to come out of your marriage. So He wants you both to be faithful so that your marriage will last. I also feel He's saying that your marriage really isn't just about you. It's about bringing the next generation of godly men and women into this world. It's not about your happiness or enjoyment—although I do believe He wants us to enjoy loving our husbands. Ultimately, though, it's about how He can achieve His purpose for the earth through your marriage.

Are you wondering...but shouldn't I be happy? Shouldn't I be attracted to and have chemistry with the man I'm going to spend the rest of my life with? Shouldn't I like him? Absolutely. I just want you to realize that isn't all there is to a lifelong, healthy, godly marriage. I'm not saying you shouldn't ask for what you truly want and desire. God's word does say that we don't have because we don't ask and that He will give us our heart's desires when we delight ourselves in Him. But I am telling you that when it comes to having a marriage that meets God's standards, you have to base it on what He says you need to make it successful. And what He says you need is faithfulness, love, and commitment. When you make the decision to marry based only on physical attraction, compatibility, and the other person's ability to make you happy, divorce is always an option because eventually those things will wane or cease altogether. But when you adopt God's attitude of hating divorce and basing a marriage on godly love, commitment, and giving, you stand a much better chance of keeping your marriage together.

Dating God's Way

Dear friends, do not believe everyone who claims to speak by the Spirit. You must test them to see if the spirit they have comes from God. For there are many false prophets in the world.
1 John 4:1, NLT

Something our church mother and fathers used to say is, "Baby, you have to try the spirit by the spirit." When I was in grade school, I had no idea what they were talking about! But when I left home and started to make a life for myself as a young adult, I understood that you have to watch people's actions, behaviors, and lifestyle, and not just listen to what they say. On top of that, you have to allow the Holy Spirit to reveal things to you that you couldn't have known on your own or that may have taken a considerably longer time for you to discover on your own.

Now let's apply this to dating. There's the way of dating that's acceptable to our society or culture. Then there's God's way of dating to courtship. I'm going to show you the difference between our world's way of dating and what God would most likely consider acceptable in dating. I say most likely because He really doesn't provide specific guidance about the concept we created called dating. He does, however, give us guidance on how to conduct ourselves in a wholesome manner that is pleasing to Him.

What our culture says dating should achieve

1) It's an opportunity to determine sexual compatibility. This one is major. Our culture is flooded with all kinds of sexual messages. I won't go into all of them here, but the one message I will cover is this supposed need to find out whether or not you're sexually compatible with someone. I'm willing to bet that someone in your life—even if they are a believer—has told you that sexual compatibility between you and your husband will be critical and may have even gone so far as to encourage you to engage in premarital sex to ensure that compatibility.

Although we've already talked about God's stance on pre-marital and extra-marital sex, I want to share my personal belief on this. I think that chemistry and sexual enjoyment is important in a marriage. But if you focus only on that, you'll lose sight of what you really need in a husband. And if you start a sexual relationship with a man who learns how to please you sexually, but has no interest in building a relationship and then a marriage with you, you're setting yourself up to be hurt and used—especially if you're looking for a serious relationship.

What I'm saying is not based on teaching you how to "dangle a carrot" in a man's face or maintain a position of power. God didn't create sex to be a weapon that you use to manipulate a man into giving you what you want. He created sex to be a good thing that's experienced in the relationship of marriage. If you can trust Him with your sexuality, you will avoid falling into the trap of having sex before marriage and viewing it as a focal point of a relationship or marriage.

2) It's just a way to have fun. The undertone of this message is "Let's just keep it casual." No rules, boundaries, or concern for the person we're dating except for what we want from them. I agree that dating should be fun because the act of getting to know another person should be fun. So often we turn it into sport or some sort of screening process. But God creates us all, and He wants us to enjoy discovering His creation.

3) It's a gateway to sex. We live in a sexually charged society. It's not just mainstream television and music that provide sexual images and messages. Our private lives are polluted with sexual behaviors and lifestyles that God never intended to exist. Pornography is now common and popular, and the sex trafficking industry is a multi-billion dollar business. We purchase and consume sex like we do food, clothing, and any other necessity and desire in life. So it's no wonder our culture thinks nothing of encouraging singles to believe that dating should naturally lead to sex, and then marriage—if it even leads to marriage. When or if you decide to take a stand for sexual purity according to God's standards, you will be in the minority until you share your own story with others who feel convicted to change and adopt a lifestyle of sexual purity.

4) It's just supposed to be casual. Remember that God's standard is sexual purity as a result of abstaining from all sexual activity outside of marriage. There's a sacredness that goes along with this because every man you meet cannot be your husband, and sex was created by God to tie two people together. Whether or not you're a virgin, once you commit your sexuality to God, you will still give your husband a sacred gift that no other man has. But in our culture, sex is treated like a commodity to be purchased, consumed, and then used for personal gratification. So in dating, you would be encouraged to have casual sex with any man you're attracted to in order to "test the waters," express yourself sexually, and gain gratification.

What God would likely say about dating

1) It's your opportunity to learn who a man is before making a commitment. When you follow God's instructions to abstain from sex outside of marriage, you stand a much better chance of really getting to know who he is and why he is requesting your time. A man who is not interested in you beyond sex or is looking for a challenging sexual conquest will eventually stop pursuing you once he realizes you are actually committed to abstaining from sex outside of marriage.

2) You should enjoy the learning and discovery process. God's way of dating centers around discovery. I found that out by reading the book of Song of Solomon. I realized something about the exchange between the young man and woman in the verses. The way they go back and forth in their conversation is indicative of two people who know each other well—and not just sexually. And you can really only know a person like that after a commitment to discovery.

Discovery is basically allowing facts about a person or life in general to unfold. It's not like an experiment where you manipulate variables. You simply take as many opportunities as you can to observe the object or person of your focus in action. It made me think of how I believe God wants us to have a "back and forth" level of communication with Him. I've had it before and it was more than fun—it was enjoyable. It was so enjoyable that I often seek quiet time and stillness so I can experience it again and again.

Notice how I said God's way of discovery is enjoyable rather than fun. Again, this is my opinion based on experiences, but I've noticed how enjoyment takes into account and respects the differences of others. Fun seems to be more selfish and self-centered.

But with dating specifically, God wants you to discover whether the man who's taking you out is the right fit for marriage or if he's not The only way you can know that for sure is if you allow the dating process to be one where you discover the man as a person and accept what you learn without reservations or justifications of red flags.

Remember when I said that God wants us to enjoy discovering His creation—to include other people? He wants that discovery in dating to be untainted by selfish motives, pre-conceived notions, and unrealistic expectations. He wants to unfold the gift of the man He's placed in front of you. All you have to do is pay attention to what's revealed to you and respond appropriately.

3) It should keep you safe. When you take the approach of dating for the purpose of getting information as you interact with a new man in your life, you keep your well-being intact. That doesn't mean you won't make mistakes while interacting with him. It means you'll be free from feeling pressured to act a certain way or do certain things to keep his attention. It means you won't feel compelled to keep dating someone who has given you reason for pause. It means that you won't fall into the trap of investing too much emotionally, physically, or spiritually too early in the dating relationship. It means you will keep your emotional, physical, and spiritual well-being first while dating men you're getting to know. It means that you'll allow God to keep you safe while you discover what He has for you.

4) It should let you know whether or not it's okay to go further. One of the gifts that God gave us was the gift of choice—also called free will. I often think Christian women get this idea that there's only one right man for them. That could be the case, but I'm open to the idea that some of the many men we meet could be great matches for marriage. So instead of asking God to reveal "the one," we should ask Him for wisdom in the selection process of our choices. During the dating process, we have a choice to accept what we see, red flags and all, or ignore the truth about what we really see. Because you picked up this book, your goal for dating should be to determine two things: whether the man you're spending time with is marriage material, and whether he's your future husband. If you find out that he's neither and you truly desire marriage, you're wasting your time by continuing to date him.

If there's one way I believe women should be like men, it's this: Men tend to determine a goal and then pick the woman who matches it. Meaning, if they want to get married, they pick a woman who they believe is right for them. If they only want periodic companionship, a lover, or "arm candy" for high profile dates and events, they'll select each one accordingly. Women, however, seem to select the man they like and then try to fit him into their goal for marriage—even if they have to drag him, coax him, or convince him. I really do think our men have it right in this aspect and we can learn something from them. The lesson being: Don't allow your affection, or even love, for a man cause you to choose counter to your desire for marriage. If you truly desire marriage, only choose a man who is suitable for you in marriage.

Part II: Now It's Time To Work on *You...*

      Now that I've shared some fundamental truths that I've learned about love, sex, dating, and marriage, I want to talk about you. In this part of the book, I want to share all the areas of my life that God has transformed. He had to change my beliefs and my heart before I could rebuild my life into one that supported my desire to marry a really great guy. So now I'm going to share how He changed me so that you can work on these areas as well.

Chapter 6: Truly Knowing God Will Change You

"Come close to God, and God will come close to you..."

James 4:8, NLT

When God comes close to you, it's hard to remain the same. If you read the previous chapter and felt like you're the least likely candidate for marriage, take heart. Deep down in my heart I believed I wasn't even though I truly desired marriage. God will teach and instruct you if you are willing to learn, and your honesty about where you are in your readiness for marriage is just the first step in actually preparing yourself for marriage.

In this part of our journey, I'll share the insights God has given me since that encounter I had with Him in late October of 2012. Now, insights aren't worth too much if you don't actually apply them to your life. So to break those insights down, I'll share the areas in which God had to change in my inner life to get me to a place of readiness for marriage during my season of singleness. These may or may not be areas you personally need to work on. But if they are, I invite you to do the work. Not only is the work designed to get you to a level of readiness for marriage; it's also designed to make you a better woman who enjoys a full and blessed life.

So let's get to work!

First, God worked on me through relationships

My relationship with God had to be developed.

Remember I said I'd made marriage an idol? Well again, Acts 17:28 tells us we live, move, and have our being in Him. He is the very life we seek. Therefore anything or any person you want more than Him becomes an idol. And idols separate you from God to the point that work has to be done to restore whatever previous relationship you had with Him.

To strengthen my relationship with God from that point (after I'd done all the things I told you to do in Part I, Chapter 3) I had to work on the following things:

1) Hearing God's voice. It's hard to hear God's voice when the desires of your heart, the voices of others, your own insecurities and cultural messages are constantly drowning it out. And I truly do believe that God's voice "sounds" different to each of us because we are different and unique. God's word tells us that His voice is a still small voice: "And after the earthquake a fire; but the LORD was not in the fire: and after the fire a ***still small voice***" (1 Kings 19:12, NLT). Whether God speaks to you through dreams, visions, people, or an audible voice, it's unmistakable because it causes you to be still. It gives you reason to pause. It's quiet and calming in a world that is noisy and confusing. And when you spend more time alone with God and reading the word, you'll develop a keener ear for God's voice.

2) Developing my prayer life.

"But if you remain in me and my words remain in you, you may ask for anything you want, and it will be granted! **8** When you produce much fruit, you are my true disciples. This brings great glory to my Father."

John 15: 7-8, NLT

I've come to understand three things about prayer. First, it's a lifeline in your relationship with God because it's communication between you and God. Second, it's a vital weapon in your spiritual warfare—for you and others. Third, it's something like an activator. It serves as a catalyst for God moving on your behalf in His overall plan for your life. He responds to the spoken words of our pleas and requests.

When I was young, prayer was not a priority and it only happened sporadically—usually when I was distressed or in trouble. And it was usually me talking to God or telling Him just what I wanted. But as He worked on me, I began wanting to know what He had to say. Then I grew to understand that it wasn't enough to know what He had to say to me, but that I had to obey in order to really strengthen my relationship with Him. Are there still times where I don't pray like I should? Of course. But I've developed my prayer life beyond touch and go requests. As a result, I can see God's nature, character, and provision in a bigger way.

Here are 3 easy ways to develop your prayer life:

First, make a habit of praying right after you get up and before you start your day. If you're not a morning person, you can keep it to just 5 minutes. Keep it simple by thanking God for allowing you to see another day, asking Him what His agenda is for the day, and then listening for a response.

Second, take breaks throughout your day to stop and pray to God. It not only keeps you connected to Him through communication, but it helps keep you quiet and still so you can hear from Him, too.

Third, make a habit of praying before you go to bed. The last communication you want at night is between you and God. It can be as simple as you telling him about what happened in your day.

3) Engaging wholeheartedly in praise and worship. Later on, I'll talk about how I found my current church home and what it taught me about knowing when a man is the right one for you. But here, I want to talk about how praise and worship will help strengthen your relationship with God. There were times in my life where I felt so overwhelmed by singleness. You know, those times where you think, "Am I always going to be alone?" or "Am I ever going to get married?" Well, those moments are the minority for me now, but when they do come, they come strongest on Sunday mornings. I push my way through, get myself together, and go to church. As soon as we have praise and worship everything changes: my countenance, my feelings of disappointment and discouragement, and my outlook. Because I decided to focus on thanking God in worship, He gave me what I needed to get through a low point.

If you have low points frequently and often feel like God has forgotten about your desire for marriage, start now in making a habit of worshipping God. "For God is Spirit, so those who worship him must worship in spirit and in truth" (John 4:24, NLT). I asked God what this scripture meant and here's what He gave me. Worship is about acknowledging who God is. And if you know God, you know you have much to be thankful for—regardless of what you think your life is lacking. So when you worship, you're making the effort to focus on how good God is. He has many other qualities, but His goodness is what you'll probably find yourself focusing on most. I say that because if you've ever sat in a chapel or church where the spirit of God was heavy, you may have felt the urge to weep (or you may actually have wept). That's because His presence is overwhelming with goodness. It's a goodness that you almost can't describe or imagine, so you weep once you feel it through God's presence. So when you worship, focus on God's goodness—not what you still want from Him. When you do that each and every time you worship, you'll find that it becomes much easier to acknowledge His goodness at other times throughout each day of your life.

4) I also developed a relationship with the Holy Spirit. This didn't happen until recently, but before I tell you how I did it, I want to explain why living in the Spirit is important as a single. There are so many traps you can fall into. We talked about loneliness and sexual temptation. I believe those are the most difficult to avoid because we're designed for human companionship and God gave us sexual desires. The problem is when we can't discern when a man only wants sex or intimacy and companionship on his terms. Then we wind up tying ourselves to and falling in love with men who never planned on committing to us. At one point before God really started to teach me about dating, I told him it seemed like I needed super powers to figure out what was going on! But of course I didn't...I just needed to learn how to have a relationship with the Holy Spirit, because he's the one who reveals God's supernatural knowledge and wisdom in real time. He's the one who can reveal things about the men you meet that you had no way of knowing on your own. And you need that so you can avoid making terrible and sometimes life-threatening decisions in the name of pursuing love.

So here's how I formed a relationship with the Holy Spirit:

I was baptized (by submersion). I grew up in a church that didn't emphasize being baptized by submersion, so I wasn't really aware of the difference between the type of baptism I did receive and baptism by submersion. I don't knock the religion I grew up in at all and I truly do believe that the baptism I received as a baby covered me in terms of salvation prior to me accepting Jesus as my savior. But the church I attend now taught me what baptism by submersion means and it was something I wanted to do simply because I wanted to be closer to God. Little did I know that it opened me up to a new understanding of and relationship with the Holy Spirit. I was already feeling his presence very strongly at times leading up to my baptism. But, like our pastor taught, my baptism was the outward act needed to activate an ongoing sensitivity to the Holy Spirit's guidance and presence in my life. Once I did, my confidence in God grew and my desire to submit to His leadership, the Holy Spirit's guidance, and Jesus' teachings increased greatly.

If you think baptism by submersion is something you want to do for the first time (or again because you felt you were just going through the motions the first time), read about Jesus' baptism starting in each of these scriptures: Matthew 3:13, Luke 3:21, and Mark 1:9.

I increased the amount of time I spend in the Word. This is a requirement to increase your relationship with each entity in the holy trinity: God, Jesus, and the Holy Spirit. By doing this you grow in knowledge, start to memorize scriptures, and gain an understanding of what you read. And that's how you grow in wisdom—the ability to make the right choices at the right time, according to God's will.

To make this a habit, you can start with a reading plan on biblegateway.com. The site has one where you can read the Bible in one year. Even if you stray for a few days during the week, at least you're holding yourself to an expectation that you will read the Bible cover to cover.

I developed an ear for the Holy Spirit's voice. I did this by determining that I was going to follow his lead. Before that, I was committed to reasoning things out in my own strength and understanding. But I finally came to a place where I said, "Okay, God...I'm tired of feeling like I'm going around the same mountain again and again. Please help me and teach me how to make choices that honor you."

This is critical in dating. I believe we live in a time where dating and making choices about men without the Holy Spirit can cost you peace, your reputation, your sexual health, and even your life. In this day, men and women don't think twice about posting personal information about someone else. If you're not careful, provocative pictures, videos, and even text messages can be shared without your knowledge and consent.

I remember there were times while I was dating that something was suddenly made clear or revealed about the man I was dating. It came quickly, quietly, and made perfect sense—and the revelation made it very easy to move on. That's what the voice of the Holy Spirit is like. He's like an agent who reveals things to you that you would otherwise have no way of knowing. Have you ever heard someone say, "Something told me to..."? That's how the Holy Spirit is. Once you start to work on yourself and your life, he'll prompt you in a way where you just know—suddenly or over time—that you need to make a certain decision.

5) Increased time alone with God. This is a requirement if you want to have a strong relationship with God. If you're not a morning person, mark off your alone time with God at night. If you're a morning person, get up an hour early so you can start your day spending time with God. Whatever time of day you do it, make a habit of doing it daily—several times a day if you can. When you spend time alone with Him, you have the opportunity to talk to Him, listen for what He might be saying to you, and just sit still with Him. You can also do something like go to a park, sit in a secluded part of your church if it's open throughout the week, or go to a designated spot in your home or work place. However you want to do it, the goal is to mark off time in your day and schedule where you focus only on Him.

My relationships with others had to be developed

Teamwork

Teamwork is the spirit at work when we come together in friendship, marriage, acquaintanceship, or another type of relationship to achieve a common goal. In order to be a team player, you have to be willing to let go of having your way all the time, be genuinely interested in helping people, and be able to follow and lead. These are all things God had to work out in my life, and I'm willing to bet you might need some improvement or refinement in one or each of the areas, too. But that's okay, because we're all a work in progress and sometimes you just don't have certain skills because you've never needed them. But you will be part of a team when you get married, and you'll need the skills I just mentioned to work well and consistently as a part of that team.

Are you part of a team now? At work? In school? In a volunteering association? At your church? Wherever it is, do your best to work on those skills that help you to be a great team player so you can walk into your marriage armed with those skills.

Communication

If you're an introvert like me, communication is something you might forget to do sometimes. Or maybe you're an extrovert and you tend to talk over everyone in any situation. Wherever you fall on the communication spectrum, just know that communication is vital to any relationship. Without it, your relationship will suffer and could even fail. Communication is a way to state needs, feelings and fears, to bond, to plan, and to exchange information. It can be written or expressed verbally or physically. Communication is the lifeline between you and God, and you and others. And when you marry, it will be the lifeline between you and your husband. Without it, you won't be able to dream together, build a life together, or just do life together.

The Bible says, "You want what you don't have, so you scheme and kill to get it. You are jealous of what others have, but you can't get it, so you fight and wage war to take it away from them. Yet you don't have what you want because you don't ask God for it" (James 4:2, NLT). We don't ask God for what we want because we don't communicate to Him what's going on in our hearts and minds that make us desire what we long for. As a result, we have to make things happen in our own strength, and just like you see from the scripture, even if we get what we want, the journey to getting it can be ugly. And so it is with communication. Things are so much easier when we can just communicate our disappointments, fears, frustrations, or even our joys to each other. We can avoid the heartache of assumptions and blaming that come from the lack of straightforward and effective communication. So in your marriage, God wants you to have clear channels of communication where you exchange information, feelings, and dreams.

Forgiveness

I can't think of many things as discouraging as trying to relate to someone who only wants to hold on to who you used to be. Have you ever had a friend, family member, or acquaintance who always wants to bring up embarrassing things you did in the past? Or they talk about "how you are" because they really don't know who you are anymore—they only know who you were 10, 15, or 20 years ago? Well, let it be a reminder that God is a transformer and that you don't have to hold on to who you were. You don't have to keep holding on to your mistakes. You can boldly tell whoever wants to remind you of the old you that God has made you a new person. Likewise, show God how grateful you are by forgiving those who have wronged you.

God also wants you to develop an allowance for others' faults and to be grateful when others have an allowance for yours. This doesn't mean that you excuse wrongdoing. In fact, God's Word encourages and commands us to deal with wrongdoings. But God wants us to live in peace with others, and we can't do that if we're holding on to grudges. So accept that no one is perfect and that they will disappoint and hurt you. Likewise with your husband, he will hurt you, disappoint you, and fail you. You'll do the same to him. You're both human. But your ability to deal with him hurting you and then let it go will help you keep a strong and healthy marriage.

My relationship with myself had to improve

Self-care and love

How well you care for yourself physically, mentally, and spiritually is the natural root of your physical appearance, your mental health, your physical health, and your spiritual health. On one of my birthdays, my friend gave me a gift certificate to get a pedicure. I thought it would be awkward, but by the time I left that spa, I thought, "What have I been *missing*?" Then I started wondering what else I needed to start doing. That alone inspired me to invest more into having professionals take care of my hair, nails, and skin. I also came up with rituals to maintain my physical health daily. Here are the things I do daily or monthly to care for my physical body as well as maintain my mental and spiritual health:

- Drink plenty of water
- Cook my favorite foods from scratch
- Eat raw vegetables and fruits
- Work out 15 to 30 minutes at a time
- Take Epsom salt baths
- Make time for full-body massages

- Get manicures and pedicures
- Spend time with friends who believe and live the Word of God
- Reach out to friends and family outside of my area
- Volunteer
- Attend church services at my church home
- Garden
- Spend time on the hobbies I love
- Play golf!

My physical appearance

Everyone's budget is different and not everyone can afford to buy and wear the newest trends and fads. Despite your budget, though, you can adorn your physical body in a way that reflects how good you feel about yourself. And I believe that what you wear (not taking into consideration the cost or brand name) often reflects what you think about yourself. When I first joined the military I really was not pressed to take time to put myself together before I left the house. I was busy—always in and out with the ship—and as a result I was tired and unhappy. Outside of work, I usually dressed in plain clothes. Sometimes I threw on flip-flops with old sweats or workout clothes. While I was in uniform I would barely comb my hair and would only do enough to make sure it was within regulations. I didn't shape my eyebrows, wear any make up, or take time for manicures or pedicures. In fact, I'd never even had a pedicure before! Not only was I a hot, single mess—I looked the part. The fact that men still hit on me is a mystery to me.

I was one of those girls who thought "I want the man for me to love me for *only me!*" and my choice in clothing reflected that. But as I matured in my relationship with God, I started to enjoy the physical parts of womanhood that personified femininity—nice hairstyles, soft clothing, accessories, and colorful shoes and purses! As soon as I found what I liked, I thought, "I've been missing out...big time!" If my experience doesn't apply to you, and you've always dressed well for every occasion, good for you. Continue to allow your clothes to be an outward expression of who God created you to be. But if you're like I was and for whatever reason you don't care about how you put yourself together before you leave the house, I challenge you now to just start choosing clothes that you love and you believe reflect who God created you to be. God created your physical appearance. Honor it by choosing clothes and accessories that flatter it.

My mental health

What works for me in terms of maintaining my sanity and mental health is making these four things a part of my life as much as possible: positive people who care about me, activities that I enjoy doing, monitoring my thought life, and taking time to sit and be still before God. That last one is key. Any time I skimp on that time alone with God, I can see the fruit of it in my life. From attracting the wrong type of man to becoming overwhelmed with life itself, living life without spending time in God's presence is much harder than it has to be. My anxiety level rises and I struggle. If you find yourself experiencing high levels of anxiety daily, depression, or any other type of imbalance, try increasing the amount of time you spend with God. What works for me may or may not work for you, but you're welcome to try it to see if it does. If it doesn't, here are more recommendations based off what I know my friends and church members do:

- Increase your daily amount of aerobic exercise
- Take breaks from working each hour
- Get fresh air for a few minutes each hour
- Watch inspirational TV shows
- Listen to inspirational music

If you've tried these things and even thought of things on your own and your mental health state is not improving, it may be time to seek counseling. Friends and family can only do so much and they don't have the training to listen to you and then help you create a strategy to actually improve your condition. If you're open to it and feel it's time to start counseling, just visit chapter 10, "A Special Word For Wounded Singles."

My physical health

I love the way I feel after I work out, but I'll be honest—doing it consistently

is the hassle of a lifetime sometimes! But what keeps me committed to doing better, even when I slip up, is the fact that I know the Word says our bodies are temples for the Holy Spirit. If you really want to improve your relationship with God—or better yet the Holy Trinity—start caring for your physical body. Work out, eat well, drink lots of water, and get quality sleep. Today we're taught to go until we can't go anymore and to pack our schedules to the brim so we can get ahead in our careers. If you're a single parent you may even find yourself packing your child's schedule so they can achieve greatness, too. But just like the scripture says that we can have all these good things and gifts but none of it means anything without love, it's the same for our bodies. Our achievements mean nothing if we're barely holding on because we're always sick in our bodies. So remember to make your physical health a priority by (as I just mentioned) eating well, getting quality sleep, working out, and drinking lots of water, but also in getting regular checkups with the doctor and treating yourself to things like massages when you can afford it. Be kind to your body and it will be kind to you.

Make sure you're having routine medical checkups, too. Go to the dentist. Get your physical or bi-annual exams. If you notice changes in your body, ask your doctor about it. Get a second opinion if you feel your doctor isn't answering your questions fully or taking your complaints seriously.

Then God worked on my sensitivity to His Will for my life

I had to find contentment to receive God and His blessings

Contentment is so crucial to the quality of life you have as a single that I've dedicated a separate chapter in this book to it. But for now, I will say that contentment is key in committing to God's will for your life. When you're disgruntled, unhappy, and ungrateful, it's hard to realize the good things God has given you and to recognize and accept His will for your life. I cultivated my contentment by being honest about my desire for marriage, but also by being grateful for the other good things God gave me. That doesn't mean I didn't and don't still have bouts of discontentment. But I kept choosing not to discount the rest of my life because I was still single.

Producing the fruit of the Spirit had to become a focus in my life

Patience is the fruit I have the most trouble with. Guess why. You got it! It's often associated with waiting. And as a single woman who wants marriage, waiting and preparing can get the best of you if you let it. But here's how God got me. He showed me a vision of myself as a person in a long line at the store. In the vision, I was struggling to hold my peace while waiting for my turn to check out. And then when I got to the front of the check out lane, I wasn't even prepared to pay! I couldn't find my wallet or I'd forgotten something and had to go back—whatever the reason was...I wasn't ready yet. But I thought I was going to die standing in that long line. Isn't that a hot, single mess?

What fruit do you think you need to work on? Love, joy, peace, patience, kindness, goodness, faithfulness, gentleness, or self-control? Ask God to reveal which qualities you need to work on and then diligently work on producing them.

My God-given purpose had to be nurtured

I've heard the opinion that if God wants you to remain single, it's because he wants to use you for the Kingdom. He's given you the gift of singleness so you can live out your purpose with single-minded devotion. Well, I don't believe in the gift of singleness. I believe that only a few people (compared to the vast majority) are actually called to lifelong singleness because of God's desire to use them completely for public ministry. "But Jesus was single" or "Paul was single," others argue. Yes, they were. But they were also used in unique ways—ways that radically changed and advanced the agenda of God. Ways that were not really conducive to having and raising a godly family.

So as a single woman who desires marriage, if you're still struggling with your purpose in life, I will agree that now is a perfect time to discover it and cultivate it. I also believe you can do it in a marriage. But if the right man hasn't come along, why not start now? I'll let you in on a secret of mine. When I have moments (which are a lot less frequent nowadays) where I'm like, "God, can I please get married...before the rapture?" it helps to go deeper into fulfilling my life's purpose. I balance it out by picking up old hobbies and pursuing new ones. I know that living your life's purpose and pursuing the things you love are no match for having the right man. But they sure do make the wait time bearable and even enjoyable. Read this passage about Dorcas in the Bible so you'll see what I mean about living your life's purpose:

Down the road a way in Joppa there was a disciple named Tabitha, "Gazelle" in our language. She was well-known for doing good and helping out. During the time Peter was in the area she became sick and died. Her friends prepared her body for burial and put her in a cool room.

Some of the disciples had heard that Peter was visiting in nearby Lydda and sent two men to ask if he would be so kind as to come over. Peter got right up and went with them. They took him into the room where Tabitha's body was laid out. Her old friends, most of them widows, were in the room mourning. They showed Peter pieces of clothing the Gazelle had made while she was with them. Peter put the widows all out of the room. He knelt and prayed. Then he spoke directly to the body: "Tabitha, get up."

She opened her eyes. When she saw Peter, she sat up. He took her hand and helped her up. Then he called in the believers and widows, and presented her to them alive. When this became known all over Joppa, many put their trust in the Master. Peter stayed on a long time in Joppa as a guest of Simon the Tanner.

Acts 9:36-43, MSG

I love this story for a few reasons. I love to sew and I love how Tabitha (or Dorcas) loved what she did so much and that it helped people in real ways. When you're right with God, right within yourself, and living in your purpose, the following things *can* and *will* happen: You'll be known for what you do well; what you do well will be used practically to help others; you'll be loved by those you impact the most; people who are unsaved or weak in their faith walk will come to God because of your example. So don't discount how living your purpose can improve the quality of your life as well as that of others. Instead, get busy discovering or rediscovering your purpose and pursue it with a passion!

And last, God had to change my mind

Of course, the most important arena in your singles walk is your mindset. Here are the thought patterns and beliefs God had to address and change in me since that night He met me in Isaiah 30.

1) True beauty comes from within. Our culture values physical beauty. And I've seen and heard how many women who don't fit a certain type of beauty feel rejected and ugly. They never learn to embrace their own unique beauty and don't nurture their inner qualities. Well, God showed me that true beauty comes from within. It's like when Paul says he can have all the gifts God can give a person, but if he doesn't have love he doesn't have anything. Well, you can be the most physically beautiful woman in the world, but if your character is ugly and void of the Spirit, you don't have anything. Take the time now to work on your character.

2) Sex is a beautiful gift from God. When you start the process of trying to live for God, it's easy to fall into the traps of feeling like you'll never meet his standards or being prideful of actually being able to. What I mean is that if you've struggled with abstaining from sex prior to making a commitment to God and you still fall into it after making the commitment, you might start to feel that you'll never be good enough to uphold His standards in your life. On the other hand, if you've never struggled with abstinence, it's very easy to be prideful and believe that you kept yourself—when the truth is that if it weren't for the grace of God, you'd be sifted through like wheat (Luke 22:31). When you fall into those traps, at the root you conclude that sex is dirty, wrong, or that it's something you use like leverage or a weapon against men. You might even believe that you're better than women who can't abstain.

So wherever you fall on that spectrum, just know that sex is something God created for enjoyment and procreation between a man and a woman. Don't believe anything else.

3) Marriage is a gift from God. In general, our culture seems to have a skewed opinion of marriage. What I've seen is that we seem to think marriage is undesirable. After all, we want to be our own person all the time. And not only that, but most of us weren't taught how to work through difficulties in any type of relationship. So we abide in the relationship until it gets rocky, and then we decide to part ways because of "irreconcilable differences." Then we transfer that same attitude to marriage—that if it doesn't work out, we can just walk away and tell the judge at divorce court that we couldn't work it out.

But the truth is that marriage is a gift from God that many of us would be blessed to receive. It was designed to be a long-term relationship, only ended by death. So we should focus more on how to marry well and keep the marriage together once we do. Of course, there are serious situations where separation or divorce would be understandable, but we should cultivate the right attitude before getting married. Our attitude should be that to the best of our ability, we're getting married once and that we're going to do everything in our power (with God's help and guidance, of course!) to make that marriage last.

4) Being single isn't the end of the world. It's a requirement in order to have God's best in a marriage. Every married person you know was once single. Let that sink in for a minute. All the hoopla some of your married friends make about you still being single really doesn't mean a lot.

They were single once. And if some of them were completely honest with you, they'd tell you about their own struggles so you would better understand what other people went through prior to marriage. So if anyone who's married is making you feel as though something's wrong with you because you're still single, politely change the topic or—if necessary—end the conversation.

5) Our bodies are temples of the Lord. It seems that fast food, fast living, and fast sexual "hook-ups" are popular in our culture, too. The problem with living that way, though, is that being so quick to give of ourselves can lead us to devaluing the gifts of our minds, spirits, and bodies. Just because your other Christian (or non-Christian) friends are "doing what everyone else is doing" doesn't mean you have to do it, too. Just because you see women not valuing their minds, bodies, and spirits and still getting married, doesn't mean they did it the right way because they achieved the result you want. So honor God with your body by making choices that will save you from devaluing the gift he created it to be.

6) Men who love God or have yet to love Him *do* exist. So many women who've been single past the point they wanted to be often wonder if there are any single men left who love God. I believe there are. Check this out:

> When Elijah heard it, he wrapped his face in his cloak and went out and stood at the entrance of the cave.
>
> And a voice said, "What are you doing here, Elijah?"
>
>
> He replied again, "I have zealously served the LORD God Almighty. But the people of Israel have broken their covenant with you, torn down your altars, and killed every one of your prophets. I am the only one left, and now they are trying to kill me, too."
>
> Then the LORD told him, "Go back the same way you came, and travel to the wilderness of

Damascus. When you arrive there, anoint Hazael to be king of Aram...·

Yet I will preserve 7,000 others in Israel who have never bowed down to Baal or kissed him!"

1 Kings 19: 13-15, 18, NLT

I love this scripture. The prophet Elijah had just run away from Jezebel because she placed a death warrant on his head. Notice how in his conversation with God, he says that he's the only person left who loves God. Now, Elijah was terrified and I'm sure I would be, too. But his fear almost sounds like arrogance doesn't it? I say that because God tells him in the end of this conversation that not only was Elijah not the only one who survived this whole fiasco, but that 7,000 other Israelites held out and remained faithful to Him.

If you're caught up in the belief that there are no single men who love God, maybe it's time to take a look at your standards and beliefs when it comes to men. Yes, we should have standards, but you don't want to become prideful and snobbish towards the men you meet. You won't know a person's heart unless God reveals it to you, and you won't receive what He reveals if pride is in the way.

Likewise, if you're falling into the trap of wondering why it's so hard to meet and befriend other single, Christian women who want to live according to the Word of God, check out the "Let's Talk About It" Community at www.authorofmyfaith.com/letstalkcommunity. We meet for fellowship, to cover topics that will help you date and court God's way, and live well and happily as a single.

Chapter 7: Recovering and Rediscovering Your Femininity in a "Man's World"

I think it's funny that people actually believe that this is a man's world. I believe that if that were true, God never would have created Eve. This is my own interaction with the biblical account of the creation of woman, but let's consider this. When God created Adam, He decided it wasn't good for Adam to be alone. I'll be honest and say I have wondered if He would have even created Adam if He had created Eve first. I concluded that He would have because His heart's desire was for mankind to be in fellowship with one another. I just don't buy into the theory that women are inferior to men. I believe that it's God's order for a woman to be submitted to her husband's authority in the home, but that outside the home women are called to leadership in business, ministry, and so many other arenas for the glory of God. I believe that the subjugation of women as we know it in the past and even today is human-made, and that it is not God's best or His will for our lives.

In this chapter I want to share what femininity and womanhood is according to what I've found in the Word of God. I'll also share about who pursues whom in dating and courtship, and what our roles are as women in the body of Christ, in the world, and in our families.

A realization I had about my experiences in the military burdened my heart to talk to you about recovering and rediscovering your femininity. Women are currently the minority in the military. Once we were allowed to join years ago, we could only serve in certain capacities. Although now the majority of jobs in the military are open to women, it is still a male-dominated field. In my own experiences, I often felt overwhelmed by the culture of the Navy because of that. At first, it was so easy to get offended because I wasn't used to being around so many men at one time. I wasn't used to their sense of humor, their manner of leadership, or their relational style. After a while, I found myself—out of frustration from feeling unheard—wishing that I could just blend in instead of having the distinct characteristics of a woman.

Fast forward several years later and God began revealing to me powerful examples of woman leaders like Deborah, Miriam, Lydia, and even Esther. What I was missing, though, were the traits that made them effective as *women* in leadership roles. They were obviously valuable as women or else they would not have excelled despite the harsh treatment of women in that era.

So once I started to meditate on what it means to be a woman, I realized quickly that I didn't know what the Bible said about womanhood. So I looked up the definition of femininity on m-w.com. This is what it said:

"The quality or nature of the female sex"

When I read it, I thought, "Gee...thank you so much for enlightening me Merriam-Webster!" As you can see, unless you already know the "quality or nature" of a woman, it really doesn't tell you anything about what it means to have feminine attributes or what femininity is. So then I thought, "Well, let me look at what the Bible says about what it means to be a woman." I quickly realized that most of the examples of femininity were rooted in culturally acceptable standards of that time. I didn't want to study that for this purpose because I wanted a fresh understanding for myself that I could share with you. So then it occurred to me to start by meditating on the story of creation—specifically the creation of Eve. Before the fall, these are the distinct characteristics I noticed that Eve had:

1) She was Adam's equal but opposite representation of God in the earth.
2) She influenced Adam.
3) She was uniquely designed to help Adam achieve the mission God gave him.
4) She was that "missing part" from Adam's life.

I've heard the opinion that the serpent tricked Eve because she was the weaker of the two sexes. I don't agree. I agree that women are the physically weaker sex, but we are equal to men even though we are called to submit to them in a marriage. My opinion is that if Eve were weaker, God never would have created her. He created her because Adam was lacking something and that something was made very clear to Adam the moment he saw her. I also thought Eve wasn't weaker because Adam didn't tell her no when she gave him the apple. In fact, I don't recall the instance where God told both Adam and Eve about that tree. God told Adam before Eve was even created not to eat from that tree, and then Eve repeated the command to the serpent. My conclusion—Adam told her what God commanded. If that was the case, Adam should have reported the matter to God as soon as Eve gave him the fruit. But that's not what happened. He ate the fruit and, well...you know the rest!

Remember, this is my individual revelation so hang in there with me! But I want to keep going to show you how what I found was the exact opposite of what we're so often told about our identities as women. And what I found is this...

Eve was Adam's equal but opposite representation of God in the earth.

Genesis 1:27 (NLT) says, "So God created human beings in his own image. In the image of God he created them; male and female he created them."

This scripture doesn't say that woman was created as a smaller, weaker version of man. Or that she was supposed to be treated like a slave, child, or maid. It says that both male and female humans were made in the image of God. To me that suggests an opposite but equal representation, and perhaps both creations are needed to fully represent God, even though men and women are completely different. Each one completes the other. Yet, how many times are we made to feel as women that we are incomplete unless we have a date, boyfriend, or husband?

Eve had influence over Adam.

According to Genesis 3:6 (NLT), "The woman was convinced. She saw that the tree was beautiful and its fruit looked delicious, and she wanted the wisdom it would give her. So she took some of the fruit and ate it. Then she gave some to her husband, who was with her, and he ate it, too."

If Eve was created to be a weaker, inferior being, why did Adam eat the fruit? I'll ask that question another way. Do you do something anyone asks you to do without good reason? Do you say no to your boss? Do you always refuse to help your friends when they ask? Probably not. Why? Your boss has the power to fire you. And your friends will only take so many of your refusals in their time of need before they distance themselves from you. Well, Eve wasn't Adam's boss, but it appears that she had some type of influence over him. Why else would he eat the fruit that God told him would kill him? Likewise, you will have influence over your husband. Yet, how often are we made to feel that marriage is the last thing we want because we have to give up our ability to decide for ourselves?

Eve was uniquely designed to help Adam achieve the mission God gave him.

Genesis 2:18 (NLT) reads, "Then the LORD God said, "It is not good for the man to be alone. I will make a helper who is just right for him."

What amazes me regarding this part of the story is that right after God said this, He put the other animals in the garden that were already created in front of Adam. Then, once it was established that none of them was suitable or just right for Adam, God put Adam to sleep and created Eve from his rib. That's a point we can explore another time—perhaps in another book. But for now, I brought it up to show that God intended to make a helper that was created just for Adam. Maybe God needed to do this exercise of naming the animals with Adam so that he would recognize Eve once he saw her. Sometimes, we as God's children can't appreciate or recognize our blessings until we've had a series of what we believe were curses. Whatever God's reasons were for creating Eve in this way, Adam recognized quickly that Eve was created to help him achieve the mission God gave him—which was to be fruitful and multiply.

She was that "missing part" from Adam's life.

Genesis 2:22-23 (NLT) says, "Then the LORD God made a woman from the rib, and he brought her to the man. "At last!" the man exclaimed. "This one is bone from my bone, and flesh from my flesh! She will be called 'woman,' because she was taken from 'man.'"

I want you to take note of three things. **First, God brought Eve to Adam.** Today, that means doing the things God has called you to do through service to others, caring for yourself and others, pursuing your purpose, improving yourself, and simply enjoying your life. All of these things are discussed in this book as well. **Second, Adam realizes she's the one and claims her as his own**. He says with his mouth that "this one" is his. And check out how the NLT says "At last!" as in "Where have you been all my life? Let's go already!" **Third, Adam changes her name.** When a man knows you are different from the other women he's met, he gives you his last name.

Regaining Your Power as a Woman

Again, God looked at Adam and realized something was missing. To me, that implies that Adam was created incomplete. Let's look again at what he says about Eve the first time he lays eyes on her confirms this for me:

"At last!" the man exclaimed. "This one is bone from my bone, and flesh from my flesh! She will be called 'woman,' because she was taken from 'man.'"

Genesis 2: 23, NLT

I got so tickled when I read this because I knew I would write about it in the context of our conversation here. I pictured Adam saying to God "What took you so long, God? Finally...*finally* you brought me someone like me. Where have you been hiding her all my life?" Think about how often women believe that men would rather die than marry, or that we have to coax them into it. Look at how many women feel that they are incomplete because they're still single. I couldn't help but laugh because once again, Satan has lied and deceived us. I laughed because I found out the truth about my worth as a woman. Therefore, even though I desire marriage I know I'm still valuable even if a man *never* says about me what Adam said about Eve!

This is why if a man doesn't pursue you, he doesn't understand your worth to him. If you pursue him, you don't understand your worth either. But we'll talk more on pursuit in just a bit. Now I want to talk about what it means to be a woman, and to be feminine based off the stories of Eve, Deborah, Lydia, and Esther.

Creative

I'm a "creative soul," so this was the first feminine attribute that came to mind. But when it did, I realized that it wasn't creativity in some type of artistic or homemaking endeavor. It's the type of creativity that is birthed from being a woman born into a world that at large doesn't understand or sometimes care to understand God's true design and purpose for women. Deborah the judge comes to mind on this point of creativity.

> "Deborah, the wife of Lappidoth, was a prophet who was judging Israel at that time. 5 She would sit under the Palm of Deborah, between Ramah and Bethel in the hill country of Ephraim, and the Israelites would go to her for judgment.

> Judges 4:4-5, NLT

Once I remembered asking, "Why did she hold court under a palm tree?" I mean, even back then, didn't they have some sort of establishment for prominent members of societies to conduct business or provide services? I could be wrong. But what came to me is that because Deborah was a woman, so perhaps she wasn't allowed to sit and conduct business alongside her male colleagues. If that was the case, that didn't faze Deborah. God had given her a strong and recognizable gift. She set up shop in an area of her choosing and those who God intended for her to serve found her. They sure didn't mind sitting under that palm tree waiting for her to render a judgment on their case!

Operational Backbone

Deborah was also a prophetess. She was called to serve a man named Barak and delivered a prophetic word to him.

> "One day she sent for Barak son of Abinoam, who lived in Kedesh in the land of Naphtali. She said to him, "This is what the LORD, the God of Israel, commands you: Call out 10,000 warriors from the tribes of Naphtali and Zebulun at Mount Tabor. 7 And I will call out Sisera, commander of Jabin's army, along with his chariots and warriors, to the Kishon River. There I will give you victory over him." Barak told her, "I will go, but only if you go with me." "Very well," she replied, "I will go with you. But you will receive no honor in this venture, for the LORD's victory over Sisera will be at the hands of a woman." So Deborah went with Barak to Kedesh."

Judges 4:6-9, NLT

I believe this is another confirmation of how strong and recognizable Deborah's gifts and abilities were. Perhaps Barak didn't know Deborah personally, but knew of her reputation and abilities. Whatever it was, he refused to go to battle without her. Maybe he knew something else about her that wasn't mentioned in scripture that gave him the insight he needed to demand her company in this endeavor. If he had hang-ups about the victory going to a woman, it wasn't noted either, so I concluded that he didn't care about that. Maybe God spoke to him through that prophetic word and told him that Deborah should go with him. Whatever the case, Barak seemed to care about having the right team in place to serve as his operational backbone. Clearly this is the esteem in which he held Deborah. When you're operating in your power as a woman, this is the same esteem the men in your life will hold you in as well.

Hospitable Homemaker

Lydia came to mind on this point. Her insistence on having Paul stay with her seemed to be about making sure he was comfortable and able to focus on his task at hand (Acts 16:15). I think she may have had the gift of hospitality and making a home comfortable even though she was most likely a competent and prominent businesswoman. It shows her generosity as well. Not many people can open up their homes to those outside of their inner circle of friends and family for extended periods of time.

Influential

Men are created to be the head of the home, but women are the influencers of that home. We've covered this from the story of Adam and Eve—how Eve influenced Adam to eat the fruit from the forbidden tree (Genesis 3:6). In this case, I don't believe Eve intentionally caused Adam to fall into sin. I think she was deceived and did what women do— share what they have and know with the men and people they love. So with that type of influence comes the need to be on point spiritually because your husband trusts you to have his best interests at heart. When a man loves you with the love of God and makes you his wife, he submits to your influence over him. Likewise, when you love your husband you submit to his leadership and covering over you in your home. Why? Because God knit the two of you together and you believe that you can trust the power that comes with his role in your life. So take the time now to develop the trustworthiness in your character.

Relentless

The woman who wore out the unjust judge is the perfect example of relentlessness (Luke 18: 1-8). She had a matter that only the judge could settle. She wasn't fazed by his reputation for being uncaring and unjust. She kept pursuing the matter with him until he finally relented. She wore him out!

I've found that women have a special characteristic of relentlessness in spiritual warfare. Don't get me wrong; our brothers in Christ are strong and tenacious. But once God starts to awaken us to who we are in Jesus Christ, we become relentless! In prayer, worship, and praise, in the pursuit of justice, and in our relationship with God. We may fall off some days here and there, but once we know God's power and the difference walking with Him makes in our lives, nothing can stop us when our minds are made up.

Courageous

Esther (the book of Esther) is the perfect example—to me—of courage. We tend to believe that being courageous means that we aren't afraid. But it's the things we're most afraid of that take courage to still achieve and get through. Esther had a life-threatening ordeal on her hands. One of her husband's employees had a plot to kill the Jewish citizens of his kingdom. Esther was Jewish but her husband had no idea. So Esther's cousin helped her find the courage she needed to approach her husband—the king—to expose the plot. She did and as a result the Jewish citizens of the kingdom were saved!

Because Esther was a woman and the wife of a king who had many other wives and concubines, she had to find courage with the help of God. She could have been dismissed at best. The worst-case scenario is that she could have lost her life. However, she used the favor she had with her husband for good. I don't recall the scripture saying this explicitly, but I imagine that Esther appealed to her husband in many ways. That's why it's important to cultivate your appeal for the right man.

Appealing

Ruth (the Book of Ruth) came to mind on this. And based off her story, I saw three distinct ways that women appeal to a man who has special interest in them: by their character, work ethic, and their unique physical beauty. That man who shows special interest can see past the moments she looks a hot mess while she's working, because he sees the strength of her character and her work ethic in those moments. So the theory that you always have to be presentable in order to draw the man for you isn't true in all cases. But that man who shows special interest can also appreciate the unique physical beauty of the woman he's interested in. I believe women have a unique physical beauty that was designed to appeal to men. Some of us use it as a weapon to manipulate men and eventually bring them to ruin. But Ruth simply adorned the natural beauty God had already given them.

Ruth was a woman who didn't mind getting dirty from working hard. She worked alongside the men in Boaz's field to the best of her ability in order to support herself and Naomi (Ruth 2:2). I did some military training that helped me understand and appreciate the weight of this. I was out on a range, navigating through the woods and in a field in the middle of the day, every day for two weeks! I didn't know the sun and heat could be so taxing. I looked and felt a hot mess. So When Naomi told Ruth to clean up (Ruth 3:3) before she approached Boaz, she had good reason. Boaz had already shown special interest in Ruth. But suppose she had shown up straight from the field for their "date"? Naomi knew how hard Ruth had been working, but she also knew men and she knew Boaz. She knew that Ruth also needed to be physically appealing in order to approach Boaz and follow up on the interest he'd already shown. Ruth had already won Boaz over with her character and work ethic. The physical appeal was just an added benefit!

So remember...win his heart with your character and work ethic, but "sweeten the deal" by adorning the unique physical beauty that God has given you. That doesn't mean you have to dress provocatively or wear clothes that make you uncomfortable. But like Naomi told Ruth—wear some perfume, take care with your personal hygiene, and wear your best clothes!

Strong but Soft

As I grow in my power as a woman, I notice how the men I'm closest to now appreciate how I'm strong, but different from them. They see my softness but they don't try to exploit it. They don't hesitate to be men and protect and guide me, but they also respect the strength and abilities I bring to the party! So they see my softness, and that softness brings a certain response out of them. But at the same time, they know that I'm strong in my own way as a woman.

Chapter 8: Marriage-Minded Men Do Pursue Women

Find a good spouse, you find a good life—and even more: the favor of GOD!

Proverbs 18:22, The MSG

This chapter will be three-fold. First, I'll talk about how it's in God's order for men who are marriage-minded to pursue women. Second, I'll share some observations on the characteristics of the type of women these men pursue. Third, because I like being practical and clear, I'll share what it looks like when a man pursues you. In general, I think our culture cultivates this "free for all" attitude in regards to dating. Meaning, it's okay for women to approach men, ask them for their number, or ask them out. I suppose it is. But honestly, I've asked the question whether or not it really is and nowhere in the Word of God did I find anything that supported it. I'm open to discussion and learning more about it, but for now I'll make the case for why it's God's design for men to pursue women.

Many of us are familiar with the passage that was quoted at the beginning of this chapter. I'll include it in both the Amplified translation and New Living Translation so you can compare:

He who finds a [true] wife finds a good thing and obtains favor from the Lord.

AMP

The man who finds a wife finds a treasure, and he receives favor from the LORD.

NLT

So let's break those down a little.

The Amplified Bible says a "true" wife. Does that mean the right wife for him? Or maybe a single woman who is truly ready to be a wife? I think it's both. I think a man recognizes when you are a wife, and then when you are the right wife for him. I think as you mature in your singles walk, you'll find that the more you tie yourself to God so you can completely rid yourself of bad past experiences, the more you'll find that you're ready to receive the man who is ready for you. You'll also find that even though you're enjoying singleness, you present yourself as a wife to the right man. I know...it sounds like an oxymoron, but hang in there with me.

As we go back to the story of Adam and Eve again, let's remember that God created Eve for Adam—after He decided that Adam was in need and lacking something. Once God created her, Eve needed Adam just as much as Adam needed Eve. But in God's order, Adam was the one who verbally and physically claimed Eve as his wife. Eve wasn't the one who decided that the relationship would progress from "seeing each other" to marriage. Adam decided that. Now, this is my summation and experience with this story, but perhaps this is the essence of pursuit. Your husband meets ("sees") you, quickly and easily determines that you are different from the other women he's known, decides that you are a wife and his wife, tells you, and then your relationship progresses towards marriage.

It happened easily and quickly—Adam saw Eve and knew she was what had been missing from his life. As a result, he claimed her and gave her part of his name. Honestly, their story makes me wonder whether or not God let Adam in on what He planned to do. Because if He didn't, I think that strengthens the case that men know quickly and easily whether or not the woman God presents to them is the woman they want to marry. Here are some qualities found within the type of woman godly men want to marry.

1) They know who they are, and therefore, what they have to offer. Strong, marriage-minded men pursue women that know who they are and what they have to offer. Once you become clear about who you are and who you are not, I promise that the type of men who approach you will either be different or you'll start to respond differently to the men who normally approach you.

Confidence is key. My confidence level in myself changed when I found confidence in God and God's Word. Specifically, I found a new identity in realizing what exactly Jesus did when he died a painful, gruesome, and bloody death on the cross. Jesus gave his life for me. God pursues me *every* day. I'm not saying a man has to be like God or Jesus to have a chance with me, but I know who I am and I'm convinced of God's love for me. If I sense that a man has no genuine interest in me, I save my time, energy, and love for someone who sees and appreciates my value. Point blank.

I know I'm not perfect, but that doesn't mean that what I have to offer isn't valuable. I know it is and I would rather be single than try to be in a relationship with someone who doesn't love me or value the person God created me to be.

2) They're feminine, not seductive. Men who are looking to settle down might look at and appreciate the beauty of a woman who dresses and behaves seductively. But at the end of the day, they gravitate to women who are feminine, and who dress and behave with kindness, consideration, and class. They also make their choice for a wife based on a number of other character traits that complement who he is as an individual man—some of which they probably believe are directly related to femininity. I know it's 2014, and women are outpacing men in many ways. But I think there is value in claiming the power of our femininity. God created us as the female representation of Him, and our femininity complements men, who are the male representation of Him.

3) They have realistic standards and don't settle. I believe the key to meeting a man who meets your standards begins with forming standards that are realistic...by the Word of God. My rule of thumb is to only set standards that have bearing on a godly marriage. Meaning, only ask for character traits, values, and beliefs that will help you sustain a lifelong, godly marriage. Yes, I know you want to have chemistry and fun. Compatibility is important, too. But build your standards on the foundation you need to keep your future marriage together. We'll also talk more about how to discover standards in a new way.

4) They passionately pursue their purpose. I once saw a documentary on the missionary Heidi Baker. Early in the documentary, her husband talked about what he experienced when he met her. He'd met her right after she'd had an encounter with God and had been filled with the Holy Spirit. He said that after meeting her and seeing all the love and goodness spill out of her, he had to know more and get whatever it was she had inside of her! Now, everyone is not called to be a Heidi Baker. But stop and think about it. Wouldn't you love it if one day your husband told the story that he was so drawn to something about you that he just had to know more about you? And I'm not talking about how cute or beautiful you are, or your physique or hair. I'm talking about the gifts and character that God has placed within you that are unique to you. I'm talking about the divine purpose God placed you on this planet to fulfill. Trust me, once you discover and pursue it, the right man could pick up on it and start to pursue you!

5) In general, they're happy. If I told you about all the times men have told me that they wanted to approach me and get to know me, but were thrown off by my "serious" demeanor, we'd run out of space! But I mentioned that to share a lesson I learned. I believe that the man who is right for you will see the right thing in you will approach and pursue you. I've heard that men generally want a woman they can make happy. We know that you really can't make a person happy, so what I think this really means is that they want someone who is emotionally healthy enough to be happy with themselves and their lives, and consequently with the man they choose. Therefore, who he is, what he does, and what he has to offer will make you happy. I've also heard that if you're a miserable single, you'll be a miserable spouse. So if you're unhappy right now just because you're single, there will come a point in your marriage where it won't make you happy. So choose to focus on how to cultivate joy in your everyday life so that once you receive more, you're already grateful and happy.

6) They're no stranger to fun and laughter. "Heaven-throned God breaks out laughing" is a phrase from Psalm 2:4 (The MSG). I think laughter is a part of God's response to us that we miss in the scriptures. When I saw this scripture, I was shocked that God laughed! Then I broke out laughing trying to picture what God "looks" like laughing. But the understanding I walked away with was that God created us in His image, therefore He wants us to find the enjoyment, amusement, and sometimes irony in things that cause us to erupt with laughter.

In the context of this scripture, it is kind of ironic to me that God laughs in response to what was said about Him in verses 1 – 3 in Psalm 2. To laugh in response to accusations or lies shows strength of character and surety of being. God knows who He is and doesn't need to prove it! Yet, He still gives us opportunities to know who He is. Likewise, I also believe a woman who can laugh at herself, the circumstances she faces in life, and even the lessons she receives from God is a woman that the right man can definitely appreciate. She can allow people to get to know her without constantly having to prove herself. And she doesn't let the ills of life steal her joy.

7) They are active. Men get bored with us, ladies. And not for the reasons you think—like being an introvert, dressing a certain way, or having a certain job. It's usually because we don't have a life or interests outside of work and church. Active women engage in life activities that expose them to interesting people and opportunities to expand their social circle. I'll use myself as an example. I've already said that I'm an introvert. I love people, but I've never been one to have a lot of friends. In spite of that, I've taken advantage of many of the opportunities to broaden my life experiences and meet new people. Through the Navy, I've been to Israel and "walked where Jesus walked." While I was stationed in Okinawa, I traveled to Hong Kong and mainland Japan. While I was stationed in Djibouti, I went to Kenya, Tanzania, and Uganda. If there's a hobby I want to learn about (like sewing, painting, or cake decorating), I do it. Whether or not I keep it up is another story, but I do it! Recently I've taken up golf and fully intend to keep going with it. And when I'm not tied up with work, I like to volunteer and hang out with the new people I meet through work, church, and other organizations.

Is there something you've wanted to do or try? A place you've always wanted to visit? Do it or go now! I know you might want to wait so you can share the experience with the right man. But if he hasn't shown up, look at it this way...if you take every opportunity to have new life experiences now, you'll have quite a story to tell him about yourself when you finally meet. So take that class. Plan that trip. Go to the networking event you saw advertised. Do it now so you can become active and start living your life fully.

8) They allow a man to pursue them. Some men are just nice guys. I'll admit that some men, who I've never even dated, have me spoiled. They were just so nice to me, thoughtful and chivalrous. I knew better than to confuse good home-training with special interest in me. But at the same time, I thanked God for allowing me to know what it feels like to be treated well by a man who wasn't related to me. And after a while I had no problem letting them be kind and chivalrous. And when I verbally expressed my appreciation, it was well-received.

So the man who is pursuing you because he's interested in you would also want you to be receptive to his attempts and wants to make sure that his efforts are not in vain. I do believe that a man will pursue until he feels there is no chance. But even still, he's not trying to let you get away. So the more you allow him to pursue you, the more he will fill a leadership role in your life and take every opportunity to demonstrate that you're the one he wants in his life.

9) The man feels better for being around her and having her in his life. When you have the right standards, the right man will actually love that about you. And you should not be prideful about it. I think the reason we miss the mark so badly when it comes to having standards is because we either have unrealistic standards or we become prideful about having the right ones. You will most likely lose a real man who is right for you if you do either of those two things. But when you adopt God's standards and adopt an attitude of humility (as in you're humbled that God has given you the opportunity to live to His standards), the right man will feel that he has a chance to have a relationship with God if he doesn't already have one, or he'll feel that you take his own standards to the next level.

10) They are secure in their singleness. In general, I've noticed that men who pursue women pursue the ones who aren't desperate for male attention or marriage. They are content where they are. Even when they share that they desire marriage, it's not done in a way where the man feels pressured about it. He either is the one or he isn't. And in the process of dating and learning about this new person, the woman doesn't feel the need to prove her worthiness for his attention. You can deeply desire marriage, but not be driven to desperation because you don't have it. We'll talk more about contentment a little later on.

11) They're not tied to their past. If you are a woman who has made choices that have negatively impacted your life, you have to heal and learn to move on or live with the permanent consequences in order to have all that God has for you. Once you heal, learn from the lessons they taught you. If it comes up in conversation, the right man for you won't be intimidated by certain things in your past like homosexuality, promiscuity, drug abuse, sexual assault or sexual abuse, domestic violence or other serious issues.

That being said, I think the key is to know when to bring these things up and to believe that you are not your past. You may still be living with the consequences of decisions you've made. But if you are in Christ, you are a new creation. And if the man who's consistently requesting your time, attention, and presence is the right one, I believe the Holy Spirit will reveal when it's time to share parts of your past with him. Until then, don't believe that you don't deserve a good husband because of mistakes or poor choices. So untie yourself from your past by learning who you are in Christ and letting God heal you.

Chapter 9: Contentment...The Perfume That the Right Man Will *Never* Forget

"But godliness with contentment is great gain." 1 Timothy 6:6, KJV

"How can I be content being single, when the only thing I can't seem to do is get married, God?" That seemed to be my heart's cry for a very long season of my life. Mind you now, for a large part of my young life, I was not pressed about marriage. I wanted the romantic love I saw in movies and novels, but I was not sold at all on the idea of marriage. But one morning I woke up with this nagging feeling that I was missing out on something. I'd never had that feeling before and it wore me down. At first, I thought I missing marriage and children. So naturally the fact that marriage and children hadn't happened yet slowly started to stress me out. Friends and family members asking me—sometimes in mean, hurtful ways—why I was still single didn't help the situation. I became exasperated. Thank God I didn't act that frustration out by pursuing men. Men have a way of spotting desperate women a mile away! But I did question God relentlessly about why I was single when He let other people get married. And we all know how that ended, right? In God meeting me in Isaiah 30 and reminding me that nothing and no one was supposed to take first place in my heart—that number one was reserved for Him only.

So now I want to show you what I learned about contentment: what it is, what it is not, and how to cultivate it. I also want to start with why contentment is such a crucial part in your ability to attract the right men, especially once you've hit the age where you thought you'd be married but you're still single.

Why you need contentment

Contentment is the state of being grateful for the good things you have—even if you have deep desires for things you do not have. Again, the scripture tells us that godliness plus contentment creates great gain. I believe that means even if you've mastered the areas we've already discussed and continue to do so in your singleness, it won't mean too much of anything if you can't cultivate contentment for where you are. More specifically, if you can't be grateful for the provision that God is providing in other areas of your life simply because you don't feel He's answering your prayers concerning a husband, that will make you ungrateful for what He has given you.

And I'll let you in on a secret. Most women who married God's way and did it later in life have revealed that they reached a point of contentment at some point before they met their husband. Now, I'm not saying that contentment is some magic activator that draws the right man to you. I don't believe that. But I do think that it greatly increases your quality of life. You feel at peace. You're open to what comes your way. You don't have to have your way in order to be happy. You even smile more. And think about it. Think about the last time you were just so content with where you were. Didn't it make even unbearable circumstances bearable? So I pondered on why contentment seemed to occur before each of these women I just told you about met their husbands, and even asked God to increase my understanding of why based on His word, and here's what He gave me. ***Contentment is the perfume that the right man will never forget!***

After He revealed that to me, I thought about His heart as a father—one who likes to give His children what they ask for. I questioned Him about that, too. I asked, "Well, if you revel in giving us what we ask for, why do so many of us remain single when we really desire to be married?" He reminded me of Jesus' teaching that often when we ask, we ask amiss. In this case, meaning we ask with ungrateful hearts, the wrong motives, and with no understanding of what we're really asking for. Then I had a vision of a father who had several daughters. One always did what he asked with no complaining. One sometimes did what he asked, and complained loudly if it was something she didn't want to do. The third was the problem child. She didn't appreciate anything her father did, complained about anything she was asked to do, and felt entitled to whatever she asked for. The father loved each of them equally and withheld nothing from them. But which child do you think the father would be most likely to grant a special request to? If you're not sure, and you're a child in a family with multiple children, ask your parents or caretakers and see what they say! But I'll tell you that through that example, God showed me that the daughter whose heart condition was right towards her father was the one who was most likely to receive a special request.

Now, God does give us blessings we don't deserve. So there's no hard and fast rule that God withholds things you're absolutely not ready for. But I'm saying that most women who were married God's way to men who were great matches for them were content, but still hopeful that marriage would happen in God's timing and in His way. They didn't allow self-motivated fears or badgering from well-meaning (or even mean-spirited) people to make them desperate to get married. They found a way to be grateful for the advantages of being single while still maintaining hope that God would prepare them for a godly marriage.

That being said...

Contentment is...

Not taking disappointment personally. Meaning, you work through your feelings about not being asked out on a second date when you thought you both hit it off. You don't automatically assume something is wrong you when you go through seasons of not dating. You realize that everything will not go your way all the time. It means you can acknowledge your disappointment and find a healthy way to work through it.

Counting your blessings. God can handle you giving him a negative confession—one where you admit you're lonely, you're afraid you'll never get married, or you feel like He's holding out on you. But even if you fall into negative emotions and communicate them to Him, God still loves for you to count your blessings. When we're content, it doesn't mean we ignore how we feel when we realize that we're missing something we desire deeply. It means we have the ability to realize that God has still blessed us with so many other good things. It means we still have the ability to thank God for what we do have.

A signal to the right man! Contentment sends a clear message: that you are mature and have the ability or at least the drive to deal with all that life brings. When you're content you're often smiling. And not just a phony smile, but also the one that comes from within. It's a state of being that communicates "I accept who I am, I enjoy (or find a way to) enjoy my life. And I trust God." The right man is going to see that and want to figure out what is going on with you, or why you seem different from other women he's met. And when he finds out, be prepared to get to know him and stick it out for the long haul! It may not go in that direction, but the man who is right for you will notice your inner shine from contentment above your physical qualities.

Contentment is not...

Fooling yourself into believing you don't want marriage. That's denial. Denying that you want to get married won't make you content. It surely won't move you closer to the actualization of your heart's true desire—to get married and stay married. Ignored discontentment and frustration will only yield bitterness, which will make you believe that you don't want marriage or that you're done with dating.

Ignoring bouts of dissatisfaction and discontentment. In fact, your ability to recognize, accept, and work through those bouts of discontentment are what helps you move closer to contentment and adopt it as a lifestyle. I think people who pursue happiness pursue something that is very fleeting because happiness is often based on having the ideal life circumstances. But pursuing contentment means you accept all that life brings you, even if it's something you didn't want or plan. So when you accept that you don't have everything you want when you want it, but can still focus on the good things you have, you're able to live a lifestyle of contentment.

So the exact opposite of contentment is desperation...

Desperation is a foul stench that attracts all the wrong types of men and repels the right types of

men. When you're desperate, you're so bent on having what you want immediately that you disregard logic, your conscience, or even caution from friends and family. You disregard the Holy Spirit's prompting in your own spirit. And that's what makes desperation like a foul stench that attracts only the wrong types of men—the ones who will stand you long enough to get what they want and then leave you high and dry like they never even knew you. And the men who are looking for marriage (or at least would marry the right woman once they met her) want someone who has standards. So when they sense desperation, they actually turn and run the other way!

Here's how to cultivate contentment...

1) Count your blessings. Sure, you don't have everything you want in life. And this is not to minimize your desire for marriage and family. But do you have a safe home? Food to eat and clean water to drink? Clean and quality clothing? Friends and family? A loving church home? A job to support you financially? Then believe it or not, you have more than many people in the world. I saw this firsthand during my time in Djibouti, Africa. The first time I left the camp I was almost in tears when I saw the living conditions that the majority of the country lived in. The vast majority had limited or no access to living water, some lived in tin huts, others lived in remote parts of the country with no sign of civilization for hundreds of miles. The part that really broke my heart was volunteering in an understaffed orphanage. I'll just say I didn't have the heart to go back and volunteer again. But that experience changed me for the better. Whenever I have serious bouts of discontentment I remember to count my blessings and remember that I have more than many people in the world have. Therefore, I should thank God despite any unfulfilled desires and act like I'm blessed!

2) Reach out to those who love you. Reach out to them and let them fulfill your need for human fellowship and relationship. We weren't created or destined to live alone. Sometimes discontentment comes from loneliness. Loneliness is a part of the human condition because no other person can completely fill the void you have in your spirit, body, or being. Only God can do that. But sometimes loneliness can be an indicator that you just need to reach out to the people you do have in your life who love you. People who truly love you will respond in kind, spend time with you, lift your spirits, and give you the opportunity to pour into their lives. If you don't feel you have those types of connections yet, we'll cover how to meet new people and cultivate those relationships. But if you do, reach out, re-connect and create new memories to help you through the next time you feel discouraged or discontented.

3) Draw closer to God. The scriptures tell us to draw close to God and He will draw close to us. I did that by reading scriptures about the life of Jesus in the New Testament. Jesus' life was the best of example of how our relationship with God can sustain and satisfy even in discouragement, heartbreak, discontentment, and loneliness. And don't just read it. Really look for clues left by Jesus' life about how you can have the same fellowship with God. After all, He wants to be the love of your life and remain the love of your life even when He gives you that awesome, special, godly husband!

If you are seriously struggling with discontentment and discouragement, I want you to meditate on this scripture:

> Psalm 16: 5-6: "LORD, you alone are
> my inheritance, my cup of blessing.
> You guard all that is mine. The land
> you have given me is a pleasant land.
> What a wonderful inheritance!"

At the core of contentment is a heart that trusts God. It's a heart that knows that no matter how things work out, God has your best interests at heart. So often we fall into despair, desperation, and discontentment because we believe the enemy's lies that God doesn't care about our desires and that there's no hope.

Now let's pray for contentment to take root in and grow in our hearts:

Lord Father God,

Thank you for all that you've done for us. Help us to grow in wisdom so that we understand that even if you never did anything else for us, you've already done more than enough. We pray right now that you remind us every day that you are good and that you love us. In fact, you love us so much that you allowed Jesus to die a horrible, inhumane, and gruesome death on a cross—like a criminal. You allowed Jesus to make us right so that we would have a right to the tree of life and so that we could have an abundant life here on earth. Help us to see that we have so much to be grateful for. Help us not to allow the things we don't have to disquiet our hearts and lead us into developing ungrateful spirits. Help us to have that fine line between maintaining hope that you will fulfill our desires and placing those desires into your capable hands—daily.

This we ask in your son Jesus' name.

Amen

Chapter 10: A Special Word for Wounded Singles

This chapter is dedicated to single women who have experienced trauma and hardship early in life. To be specific, I'm talking about rape, molestation, abandonment, bullying, witnessing domestic or neighborhood violence, and ongoing abuse. I've met people who have overcome serious issues like these and gotten married without committing their lives and healing to God. But each of them still struggled in that relationship because they constructed their own idea of what their lives and marriage should look like. They had partners who tolerated their dispositions and basically just went along with their learned behaviors and attitudes.

That's not what God wants for you. How do I know? Because I fell into that category until God confronted me about it that night I was reading Isaiah 30. I didn't mention this part in the previous chapter, but out of that encounter came an understanding that my perception of God, life, myself, and marriage was colored by certain experiences I'd already had in life. I won't go into detail here—I know that part of my journey is for another book! But I will say that I know many of us stay single longer than necessary because our wounds go unhealed. As those wounds go unhealed, we are mentally, spiritually, and emotionally closed to God in one or many ways and miss out on His healing process. We miss out on opportunity after opportunity to love and be loved because we don't want to get hurt again. All the while, we don't see that we've become someone who repels the very things we want—commitment, love, community, marriage, and family.

So I want to give you some practical exercises, recommendations and resources to help you uncover the unhealed wounds in your life so that you can heal and move on. It's a simple three-step process to get you started:

1) Identify the hurt.
2) Understand the truth about what happened.
3) Create strategies for healing and growth.

It may not be easy. But I will help you through the process and even help you identify local resources to help you stay the course. So here we go:

Identify the hurt:

1: Identify the wound.

      Who hurt you? What happened? When did it happen? How do you believe you see yourself, life, others, and God as a result?

_____

_____

_____

_____

_____

_____

2: What negative emotions are you dealing with or have you struggled with as a result?

_____

_____

_____

3: How do you feel about the person or people who hurt you? The people who allowed it to happen? Or those who knew, but didn't try to help you after the fact?

_____

_____

_____

4: Do you think you're able to forgive those who wronged you or played a part in it?

_____

_____

_____

Understand the truth about what happened:

1: Why do you think that happened to you?

_____

_____

_____

2: What do you think God's Word says about bad things happening to children or people who didn't provoke wrongdoing?

_____

_____

_____

3: What do you think and feel about God's role in what happened to you?

_____

_____

_____

Create strategies for healing and growth:

1) Seek counseling.

You don't always need counseling. But if you've suffered one or multiple traumatic and life-altering events and you suspect that any of them are causing you to respond negatively even to good things in your life, you need to consider counseling.

One of my hopes is to become a licensed professional counselor. I've almost completed the coursework and have always loved psychology. Based off the training I've had so far, I know firsthand how counseling can help you rebuild your thought life and emotional life—just like we've done up to this point. So I'm an advocate of the counseling relationship and process, and want to assure you that it is designed to provide a safe place and a safe relationship to help you build on the work we've done here together.

How to find a counselor:

Use Google.

You can find anything on the Internet today, so Google is a great tool to find counselors in your area. But use caution. Just because you find their information on the Internet doesn't mean that you have to use their services. Just search for the information on Google and collect a list of counselors you think you'd be interested in.

Ask trusted friends for referrals.

This is the same thing as searching on the Internet, except you have the word of someone you trust to go by. Referrals are great because they can save you time in the search. But remember that what works for the person who referred you may not work for you. So add these referrals to your list that you've already compiled from your Google search.

Interview your leads.

This is what will help you actually make the decision on which counselor is right for you. Ask them for their credentials, the theories they base their treatment on, and whether or not they have to report progress to your healthcare provider. If their fees are too much, ask them if they have a sliding scale fee. The interview is the time to gather as much information about your counselor as possible.

Pay attention to how you feel during the interview.

If you don't like the way this person talks to you, how they describe their treatment process, or their demeanor, don't select them as a counselor. Move on to the other options you have on the list you've compiled. The counseling relationship should be a safe place. Yes, a good counselor will challenge you and not allow you to remain stuck in bad, self-destructive, or ungodly behavior. But they also will not demean you or treat you harshly in the process.

2) Now consider...who do you have in your life that is safe to talk to?

A pastor, close friend, relative, or church member? You don't have to disclose what happened, but perhaps you can ask them to pray for the symptoms you've been experiencing as a result of what's happened to you. Use this space to list the safe people in your life.

_____

_____

_____

The truth about your wounds and your mistakes

So now I wanted to take a moment to talk to you about what you might believe about your mistakes or your past. I think it's common for women—and men—who grow in their relationship with God to believe that God won't bless them with a good, quality spouse because of their past or their mistakes. I can understand where the belief would come from. God does challenge and teach us in the Word to live an upright and moral life. Consequences for our disobedience are very clear. But I want to go back to a scripture I used earlier in the book. "You must worship no other gods, for the LORD, whose very name is Jealous, is a God who is jealous about his relationship with you" (Exodus

34:14, NLT). I used the NLT here to show that God's focus in His jealousy is over His relationship with you. While your sin will separate you from Him, it's not what He wants. He wants you to stay close. And even when you stray in the worst way possible, He still loves you and wants you back. The only thing that can keep you from God permanently is your refusal of Him and Jesus Christ.

Let's take a look at this story so we can get an idea of God's heart—through the example of Jesus Christ—for women who have made terrible mistakes:

> Jesus went across to Mount Olives, but he was soon back in the Temple again. Swarms of people came to him. He sat down and taught them. The religion scholars and Pharisees led in a woman who had been caught in an act of adultery. They stood her in plain sight of everyone and said, "Teacher, this woman was caught red-handed in the act of adultery. Moses, in the Law, gives orders to stone such persons. What do you say?" They were trying to trap him into saying something incriminating so they could bring charges against him. Jesus bent down and wrote with his finger in the dirt. They kept at him, badgering him. He straightened up and said, "The sinless one among you, go first: Throw the stone." Bending down again, he wrote some more in the dirt. Hearing that, they walked away, one after another, beginning with the oldest. The woman was left alone. Jesus stood up and spoke to her. "Woman, where are they? Does no one condemn you?" "No one, Master." Neither do I," said Jesus. "Go on your way. From now on, don't sin."

John 8: 1-11, MSG

If that wasn't a moral failure, I don't know what was. And to make it worse, she was exposed in public in front of a mob that seemed bent on witnessing the consequences of her actions. The part of this story that embodies God's attitude towards sin and His love for the sinner is quite clear. First, we are to remind one another that none of us has upheld the law totally and completely. Second, it's the sin that is to be killed—not the person. Third, what matters is that the person doesn't continue doing what they did. I find it so sad when Christian leaders are exposed in public over moral failures. I believe that God holds leaders to a more demanding standard, but that ultimately He is the one to judge—not us.

I believe that the adulterous woman is more like you or someone you know than you realize. I'll offer this to you. How many children do you think grow up saying and thinking in their hearts "You know, one day I want to grow up and be an adulterer, murderer, a prostitute, drug abuser, alcoholic..."? I'd argue that none do. I believe when serious character and moral failures occur, you can usually trace it to something traumatic or unfortunate that happened to them. Otherwise, they may have grown up witnessing it and therefore believed it was normal and acceptable.

God knows the truth concerning what happened to you. He also knows the truth about the choices you've made as a result. Nothing you've done can disappoint Him so much that He never wants you back. So if you suspect that old wounds have left you angry, untrusting, and bitter, take the time now to heal before you go out on your next date. I don't believe you have to be healed completely before you date and meet the right man. Just like I don't believe all of us will be 100% ready to marry that right man. But I do believe that leaving certain emotional and mental issues unhealed prior to meeting the right man can keep you from going further in that relationship. Even if your unhealed pain doesn't stop the relationship, you'll have to deal with unnecessary issues that could have been avoided.

Let's pray:

Lord,

Life happens. Your Word says that the rain falls on the just and the unjust. That we should not be surprised when trouble comes our way. But some things are hurtful and we cannot make sense of why they would happen to us or to anyone we love. They hurt so badly that it takes so long to get over them. And they leave us not wanting to love or trust ever again. But God, we know you created us to live in marriage, community, and fellowship with one another. Revive, restore, and heal our hearts so we can love again, hope again, and trust in you fully again. Everything we are was made by and for you. So we place our hearts back in your hands.

This we pray in your son Jesus' name. Amen

Part III: Build Your Dating Life to Please God and Marry His Best!

This is the *fun* part of this book! Now that we've discussed addressing and correcting (if need be) your current beliefs and attitudes, and how to strengthen your innermost being, now it's time to talk about making new friends, actually dating God's way, and how to know whether or not the men you meet are a match for you.

Here, I'll share what types of friends you want in your inner circle (as well as those you don't), a little on how to get out and make a life for yourself, the general categories of men and how to interact with them according to the category in which they fall, and insights on how to date in a way that pleases God. Once you learn these things and adapt them to your personal life, you'll see the men you meet in a whole new light. Most importantly, you'll see your life in a new light.

Chapter 11: You Become Who You Hang Out With

Become wise by walking with the wise; hang out with fools and watch your life fall to pieces.
Proverbs 13: 20, MSG

Part of your success as a single begins with the company you keep. When you're in between dates, it's your friends, community, and inner circle that will keep you uplifted. When you're discouraged, they'll make sure you keep going. And when you're about to cave in, they'll keep you on track and grounded. And when you get married, they'll be at your wedding and part of your community that supports and sustains your marriage. They'll also be the ones you reach back to mentor in dating, romance, and then marriage.

It's not Christ-like to judge people and decide who's worthy of your friendship based on your own understanding. That being said, God will not reward you for making poor choices in friendship either. If you sense Him revealing to you that you shouldn't let certain individuals into your inner circle, yet you let them inside anyways, don't be surprised if they wreak havoc on your life with betrayal, giving you ungodly advice, or providing a bad example for you to follow. On the other hand, if you sense God giving you compassion for someone He doesn't necessarily want in your inner circle, He could be calling you to witness to that person or just be His hands to show loving kindness. Jesus himself spent a lot of time around people who had questionable character with the goal of ministering to them, healing them, and teaching them his father's will. He also had his inner circle of disciples. Beyond that, his closest fellowship was with God.

"The disciples had their own issues, too," you might say. That's absolutely true. I do think, however, that each disciple had a specific purpose in helping Jesus bring God's will to fruition in his life—whether that role was positive or negative. In your life, though, we want you to have an inner circle of friends who help you to be part of a community where they can pour into your life and you can pour into theirs. They help God's will come to fruition in your life; they don't hinder it. They won't be perfect. Sometimes they won't be there for you. There could be periods where you don't hear from them or spend time with them. They may even let you down. But in the end, you'll be connected for a season or several, or maybe even a lifetime because God ordained it to be so.

I can tell you from experience that there are some people you want in your inner circle and those you do not want in that circle. I want to illustrate this point by using profiles of women in the Bible.

First, let's start with the women you want to invite into your inner circle...

Lydia

> "On the Sabbath, we left the city and went down along the river where we had heard there was to be a prayer meeting. We took our place with the women who had gathered there and talked with them. One woman, Lydia, was from Thyatira and a dealer in expensive textiles, known to be a God-fearing woman. As she listened with intensity to what was being said, the Master gave her a trusting heart—and she believed! After she was baptized, along with everyone in her household, she said in a surge of hospitality, "If you're confident that I'm in this with you and believe in the Master truly, come home with me and be my guests." We hesitated, but she wouldn't take no for an answer."

Acts 16: 13-15, MSG

By this passage we also know that she was a hospitable woman and a woman of prayer. These are two characteristics you will need in a friend. You need someone who will welcome you into their home both physically and spiritually, and who will be on your "prayer team." If you really want to see your singles walk go to the next level, find friends who will pray in the Spirit for and about you.

Another great thing about Lydia is that she was connected to a larger group of women. Period. If you're a woman who doesn't easily connect with other women, don't believe the lie that women just don't get along. I believe that is a rumor started by a woman who doesn't have the emotional maturity to get along with anyone else! I know some of us can be harsh towards one another, but many of us still truly desire to get along with and connect with each other. So if you don't know how to connect with other women in meaningful ways, seek out a friend like Lydia who can usher you into a network of strong, mature, and godly women. Lydia seemed to be a strong force or a leader among a group of women who came together for the same spiritual purpose. Sometimes all you need is a mentor to show you how to relate to other women in a new and meaningful way.

And let's not forget that Lydia was a businesswoman. She was a seller of purple cloth, which means she may have had "high-end" clientele. That's no easy feat for a woman who very well could have been single or widowed in those times. As a successful businesswoman, your Lydia will also have valuable insights on how to conduct yourself in other relationships in your life: professional, personal acquaintance, and otherwise. And going back to her possibly being single...whatever Lydia's reason was for remaining single, she didn't seem to be bitter as she was God-fearing and later on filled with compassion due to the Holy Spirit. So while your Lydia may not be able to share insights on how to date with the purpose of marrying, she may have insights on the character and nature of men that can help you navigate the world of dating and romance.

Ruth

"But Ruth said, "Don't force me to leave you; don't make me go home. Where you go, I go; and where you live, I'll live. Your people are my people, your God is my god; where you die, I'll die, and that's where I'll be buried, so help me GOD—not even death itself is going to come between us!"

Ruth 1:16, MSG

I believe we were created for relationship. I believe that because God is a triune God. In Genesis 1:26 when He said, "Let's make people in our image," I thought, "Who was He talking to? Jesus and the Holy Spirit?" Perhaps. But that's when I realized He's a God of relationship. And that's why life is so much better when we're not in a state of unhealthy codependence on or antisocial independence from others. Deep, abiding relationships with loyalty, understanding, and friendship are vital to our wellbeing. We may get by in life without them. But honestly, at what cost?

I believe we all do well to have just one or two Ruths who stay with us during our lifetime. Ruth was loyal and somehow probably knew that God had arranged her relationship with her mother-in-law, Naomi. Naomi's husband and their two sons had died, leaving her widowed with her two widowed daughters-in-law, Ruth and Orpah. After their deaths, Naomi made the decision to travel back to her homeland. I say that Ruth probably somehow knew, because when Naomi started the journey back home with these two young women, she told Ruth and Orpah to go back to their homeland for a greater chance of remarrying. Orpah turned around and went back. Ruth wouldn't hear of it. Ruth said that not only was God her God, but that nothing was going to separate the two of *them*!

In your life, allow God to show you when a Ruth is supporting and befriending you. Allow God to guide the two of you in your sharing and the time you spend together.

Naomi

While Naomi was very bitter over the death of her husband and sons and almost discounted Ruth entirely early in their journey back to Jerusalem, Naomi was also responsible for ensuring Ruth's destiny. Naomi represents the spiritual mother or mentor who will give you *godly* advice in the matters of dating and courtship. She can tell you the detours and dead ends to avoid. She'll be your biggest supporter and cheerleader as you date and journey on to courtship. You'll never find her giving you guidance that "keeps you single." If she's married herself, she can tell you how she met her godly husband and the do's and don'ts she adhered to during her courtship. She's the one who can walk you through areas of confusion when you tell her what's happening with particular men you're dating. If she's unmarried, she can give you godly advice on how to keep yourself in God's way on your own single's walk.

Your Titus 2 Women (Titus 2: 3-5)

I said Titus 2 women because you want both the older and younger women that are described in this passage to be a part of your life. In my church, I'm part of a life group with "Ruths" and "Naomis." They are both leaders, but the Naomis are the older mentors, while the Ruths are the younger mentors. This made me think of the Titus 2 woman, but when I revisited the passage, I noticed that the older woman was mentioned along with the younger women. It's kind of like Ruth and Naomi, except there were multiple women. The Titus 2 passage made me think of living in a community of women who mentor and learn from each other.

The older Titus woman is a woman who can actually help you prepare to marry God's way and keep your marriage together because they actually did it. This is important. Why? Because at some point in your singles walk, if you really want to cut your "learning curve" in half, you should seek mentorship and guidance from women who have been and are where you're trying to go. As a single woman who follows God, I can offer you biblical insights and strategies in the areas of love, dating, sex, and marriage that will keep you on track so you can meet your goal of being found by Mr. Right. But those older Titus 2 women are the ones who have arrived where both you and I are trying to go! They add a totally different element called experience to the mix.

The younger Titus woman is either like you in that she still believes God for a husband, she is not as far along as you in her journey, or she may be in a committed relationship headed towards marriage. Therefore, she's someone you can travel this journey with. This is good because it's helpful to share stories, disappointments, and hopes with someone who's still traveling the journey. It also helps you to remember that you're not alone and that you can also help others even if you feel you aren't where you want to be. You and your younger Titus 2 women benefit from comparing notes with each other, just like Proverbs 27:17 (NLT) says, "As iron sharpens iron, so a friend sharpens a friend."

Now let's talk about who to keep out of your inner circle...

So by now you should know that you can't do this alone. While I do believe that there are seasons in your singles walk where you won't be able to spend a lot of time (or any time at all) with friends and loved ones, I also believe that there are seasons where you will not make it if you can't allow God-sent people to help you. That being said, allowing the wrong types of people into your space will derail you. Avoid letting them into your ear or inner circle. Period.

Peninnah

Peninnahs ask "What's wrong with you that you're still single? What aren't you doing right? What did you do to make God hold out on you like that?" They're the "friends," coworkers, and family members who always find a way to work your marital status into every conversation, then talk about what you're doing to block reaching the holy grail of marriage. Don't confuse this with a friend or family member who might just want to know if you're open to meeting some really great guys they know. I personally believe that's one of the best ways for singles—especially those in their 30s—to meet people who are quality matches for them. But Peninnahs always tie your singleness to a personal deficiency. I guarantee you that if you let a Peninnah into your ear or your inner circle, you will start to doubt God. You will find yourself asking God the same questions they constantly ask you. Then you'll accuse Him of holding out on you, and you'll be right back at square one in your single's walk: disgruntled and miserable, or just wondering why you're still single.

You could do well to approach your Peninnah and tell them that their words are hurtful and cutting, and that what they're doing is not helpful. If they listen and commit to doing better, you could have some type of association with this person. But if they continue to do this to you after you've confronted them, love them from a distance. Don't commit to any type of conversation that will open the door for more, and do not spend any type of one-on-one or even intimate group fellowship time with this person.

Orpah

Although not much is mentioned about Orpah, I concluded that when all is said and done, Orpahs have no real commitment to God. I say that because even though Orpah (just like Ruth) was a foreigner who worshipped gods other than God, she had the same access to Naomi that Ruth had. Remember how Ruth said that God was going to be her God? Well, perhaps Ruth's observance of Naomi's relationship with God sparked something in Ruth that made her desire more. Orpah may have had the same type of encounter, but I don't believe she made the decision to gain more regardless of the cost. And that's a person's choice not to grow in their relationship with God. But if you have made that decision to grow closer and to increase your knowledge of God, then you cannot have this person in your inner circle.

Lack of commitment to God means their prayer life is on life support, they have no depth of knowledge of the Word of God, and their success in life is often based on the works of their own hands and not their faith in God. Therefore, they won't think twice about giving you ungodly advice. Orpah is the friend who will tell you it's okay to chase after the new man you just met. Her justification is that you don't know when you'll meet another one like him. Real friends who know God and His Word build you up and tell you that you'd be a catch for the right man. They don't tell you, "Well, you better snag that one up because you may never get another like him!" Orpah might come to church with you on some Sundays, but she's also asking you to hang out at clubs and other similar social scenes on Saturday night. Don't be surprised if at some point she walks away from the opportunity to have a real commitment to God, and any type of commitment to your friendship.

Delilah

Delilah is known for betraying Samson. But let's take a quick look at her from the perspective of what it's like to have Delilah as a friend. Delilahs are sensual and seductive. They play up their best attributes in the presence of men in order to manipulate them or just keep their attention. They're always put together, which is not always a bad thing. In fact, I encourage you to always look, do, and be your best. But Delilahs often do it with the intention of seducing a man and that is not what you want on this journey. If you hang out with a Delilah long enough, you'll pick up her habits and start getting the wrong type of attention from the men you meet. Or you'll feel inadequate because you can't keep the same level of attention from men that she does. Either way, having her as an inner circle friend is a lose-lose situation.

Now, this is not to say that by association you can't minister to and be a friend to women who fit these descriptions. I believe that's what Jesus would do. I believe Jesus would treat them with love and dignity to preserve any opportunity to be a blessing. But I do not believe God wants you to become close friends with anyone who will distract you from staying on the right track. Choose your inner circle wisely. It may mean having fewer friends, but you only need true friends in your inner circle.

You also may have noticed that I didn't include the types of men you could allow to be in your inner circle of friends. I'm not against having men as friends. In fact, some of the best friends in my young life were of the opposite sex. But if you are on this journey, there's a chance that you need to change your perspective of men first so that you can have better friendships with them. Some people even believe that men and women can't just be friends. I can see the argument. While I will say I don't believe it's impossible, I do believe it requires more work to keep your heart and motives pure towards your male friends if you truly desire marriage in your heart. I have a chapter later on dedicated to the types of men I've met on this singles walk, and one of them is the type of person who makes the perfect friend for you. For now, though, let's work on building our friendships with women so that we can have strong and unbreakable bonds with our sisters in Christ!

How to find Lydias, Titus 2 women, Ruths, and Naomis...

Remember that the goal with these relationships is one or a combination of any of these things: friendship, positive association, sisterhood, mentorship, and professional networking. Although we will get to discuss the best ways to meet men who would be great matches for you, right now I also want you to be able to meet other women who can fill any of these categories of relationship I just named. When women fill these roles in your life, your life is enriched and you become a better woman by association. You also help other women become better through their association with you.

I also want to warn you...take your time when getting to know these women. Don't rush to provide personal information about yourself unless it's something you would share with everyone. Also, don't cling to one woman because you think you feel an immediate connection. The idea is to meet as many women as you can, according to God's plan and will for this season of your life. The only way you can do that is to remain open by taking your time in getting to know other women.

So here are some ways to meet these women:

Become Active in your Church

I attend New Life Providence in the Hampton Roads, Virginia area. If you go to newlifeprovidence.com, you can see for yourself the mission of the church. It's a fairly large church with several thousand members, but the leadership is always providing activities and small group ministries to help members connect. I'm an active participant in a small group, the women's prayer circle, the singles ministry, and the ministry activities for young adult women. Since I became active, I've met and connected with some awesome women of different ages, races, and walks of life. We pray for each other, reach out to one another, and perhaps one day deeper relationships will develop. Whatever comes out of it, I know I'm better by being connected to other women who help me improve.

Questions:

Are you active in a local church? If so, why not?

If so, what activities can you become involved in to help you connect with other women?

If you are not part of a local, active church, here are some ideas to find groups to be a part of:

MeetUp.com

First and foremost, this is a website so be selective in the groups you choose to be a part of. You're meeting people who have a limited or inaccurate profile to represent who they really are. Second, again—don't divulge too much personal information up front. Yet, I do recommend this website, because you can find groups of people based off a wide variety of interests, not just dating. For example, if you're active and looking for a running club for women, I'm sure you could find a group like this in your local area. It's free to you and as long as you keep your safety first, you don't have to worry about putting yourself in danger simply because you want to meet new people.

Civic and Professional Organizations

Depending on what you do for a living, being part of professional organizations that connect you to different professionals in your industry can widen your social network. I'm a Naval Supply Corps Officer, so there are organizations that promote social networking among Naval officers. I haven't found mentors this way, but I know other women who have and it worked out quite well for them.

These are just a few options. There are others like:

Alumni associations   Sororities

Neighborhood clubs   Volunteer organizations

Chapter 12: The Categories and Types of Men You'll Meet While Dating

I don't like to put men in categories or give them labels—at least not anymore! After all, labeling people doesn't help you connect with them. Most times, it gives you more reasons to alienate yourself from them. However, I do believe that men tend to fall into 3 categories of attitudes about women and marriage: one who is actively looking for a wife, one who isn't looking for a wife but is open to marrying the right woman, or one who wants nothing to do with marriage—period.

Within those three attitude categories, I've come across four different types of men in my dating experiences, and have found that many other single women come across them as well: the crook, the candidate, the contender, and the companion.

Mr. Crook (if you let him) will steal something valuable from you that you'll never get back: your time.

Mr. Crook falls into the category of the man who wants nothing to do with marriage—period. He'll steal your energy and your love, both physically and emotionally. Notice I said that he'll *steal* these things. I say that because deception, omission, or half-truths are usually involved when he's dealing with you. Even though you are responsible for giving these men your time, energy, and love, I call them crooks so you can see that you're essentially wasting valuable gifts with this guy. Once your time is gone, you can't get it back. When your energy is depleted, it takes time to replenish. When your love is abused, it can take years and sometimes a lifetime to heal. Then on top of all of that, you have to start over once you manage to break the soul tie you've created (even if you didn't have sex with him). And starting over can be difficult for you and the people who try to love you afterwards if you don't take the time to heal properly.

How to identify a crook:

Smart crooks say and do all the right things. They take you on dates they know you'll like. They engage in conversation they know you'll find appealing. They might even let you meet some of their friends or go to church with you a few times. But here are a few ways to tell that the guy you're dating is a crook and is really only looking to use you for his own benefit:

1) **He consistently tries to kiss or put his hands on you in some kind of sexual way:**
   When this happens—especially when you hardly know him—his number one priority is sex. If you can't get more than 15 minutes into a conversation before he's making some sort of physical or verbal sexual advance, he's using predatory behavior to drop your guard and desensitize you to those advances. When this happens, you can bet that all he wants is sex. It's not love at first sight. It's not off the charts chemistry. It's not natural attraction. It's a strong sign that the man you're dealing with wants you for pretty much one thing only: sex. The question is—are you willing to be a one-time conquest or the woman who's a stopgap until someone better comes along?

2) **When he talks to you, he always finds a way to reference your physical attributes:**
   I have a phrase that I stick to when it comes to physical contact in dating: "I need to see your eyes, hands, and clothes at all times during dating!" Meaning, if your eyes are always scanning my body while I'm looking at you during conversations, or you want to talk about how attracted you are to me because of my physical attributes every five minutes, it's a no-go. I'm sorry, but chances are Mr. Crook is not just trying to compliment you when referencing and blatantly looking at your body. He's reminding you—disrespectfully, mind you—what his number one priority is: to get what he wants from you. So when the references come up, find a way to exit the conversation and his physical presence.

3) **He seems more interested in your talents and abilities than you as a person:**
This is just as bad as him only being interested in what it takes to get you to have sex with him. Even if he did marry you based on the value you would bring to him as a wife and it was nonsexual, do you really want to be part of a marriage based only on performance? If he only dates you because you cook well, represent him well, or have much to offer that benefits him, what happens when you're unable to do those things? He moves on to the next woman. Then the months or maybe even years you've spent trying to get him to commit are wasted. They're wasted because you could have been using that time to hone your talents, serving the people God has called you to serve with those talents and dating men who like you for you.

4) **Every date you go on seems to be a ploy to get you isolated:**
If he consistently says, "I figured we could go to _____, then we'll just go back to my place" don't do it. Even if you're not sold on saving sex for marriage, participate in "home dates" on your terms. Don't do them unless you are one hundred percent sure that you're ready to have sex with that person. But when you are committed to God's standard of abstinence, it is hard not to act on an attraction to someone when given the opportunity, and being alone with that person you're attracted to is definitely an opportunity. So avoid this at all costs. Better yet, let go of the guy who's on this mission of wasting your time so you can move on to someone whose number one mission concerning you isn't how long it takes to get you in the bed.

5) **He calls you frequently but you never actually go out or meet anywhere:**
Now, it's possible that he might actually want to take you out on a date, but maybe he doesn't have a car. Don't deem someone unworthy of your time just

because they don't have a certain type of house, apartment, or car. But a man who is interested in getting to know you will find a way to pick you up or meet you somewhere to do something fun together. And he won't try to always find an angle to get you to drive him somewhere or pick him up. However, if Mr. Crook is in this situation with no car, he's not making plans to meet you anywhere, and he's trying to figure out how to get you to pick him up and drive him around...cut your losses and move on. Similarly, if he has a car but is willing to take up large amounts of your time on the phone without any type of face-to-face interaction, beware. He could be covering up his relationship with another woman. Or, he could just be calling you to entertain himself. Worse, it could be both. Either way, it's a waste of your time. Again, cut your losses and move on.

How to avoid a crook:

Maya Angelou said it best. "When someone tells you who they are, believe them." Crooks will normally tell you things like "I'm not ready for a commitment," "I don't want to be married," or "I just want to see how things go." When he says those things or some variation of them, believe him. And don't forget to pay attention to his actions. If he's too physical with you for your comfort, don't ignore it. The worst-case scenario is that you'll find yourself in a date rape situation. The best-case scenario is that you could wind up giving in to sex long before you ever intended to. Also, if he makes plans but falls through more than a few times early on in the dating relationship, move on. And last, if your conversations seem to revolve only around parts of you that benefit him, you're dealing with a crook. And do not assume that he'll change by your influence. You two might be able to remain friends or acquaintances, but why would you want to be associated with anyone who's only interested in what they can get from you?

One absolute way to avoid a crook is to be open and honest about your standards from the get-go. For those of you who are not yet sold on God's standard of sex only within the relationship of marriage, here's one benefit. Men who are truly interested in you will marry you before they have sex with you. Crooks will not. They know there are 10 more women who will gladly be their resource until they move on to someone else. So most crooks will disappear once you communicate the ways in which you uphold God's standard for your life. Once you gain the confidence to communicate other standards you have, crooks will most likely find a way to drop off your radar.

Candidates are men who seem to be a good fit for you, but more time and information are needed to make a final determination.

These are men who know all the right things to do and say. They take you out on dates and pay. They're respectful of your wishes and time. They want to know more about you as a person. They have a personal relationship with God. They're honest and they communicate their life goals. Even if he doesn't have a prestigious job, he is faithful to the job he has, is financially responsible, and has a good reputation with his boss and coworkers. He's made mistakes in the past and even continues to make mistakes, but he has matured and is constantly striving to be better. He's attractive to you. I could go on and on.

So then what would be the problem? Well, not every man you date is the right one for you. He could be one of several men that could be a good match for you, but you need time to determine that.

Contenders are the ones who are suitable for marriage with you.

You've discussed marriage, you have a lot in common and you share non-negotiable values. You see that you have what it takes to have a lifelong marriage. But even with contenders, be careful. I don't know if you've ever heard the theory of soul mates or the thought that God will send you that one, right man. Well, I'm of the belief that many of us will meet several men who would be perfectly good marriage candidates. So be careful that you don't rush into marriage at the first sign of compatibility. Continue to allow things to unfold at a good, safe pace and don't rush the inevitable.

Contenders are just like you in the sense that they are ready to find the right one and settle down. If he's just as anxious as you are to "seal the deal," you both might wind up ignoring red flags that marriage is not the answer for your relationship or that you need more time together before you get married.

But let's say you really do believe in your heart that this contender is the one for you. Make sure you closely follow the recommendations I have for you in the dating chapter in Part III of the book. Above all else, find local mentors who you trust to be your confidants and advisors during your dating relationship and courtship. Let your contender meet your friends, mentors, family, and church family. That way, they know they are part of a community of people who want to see your relationship and eventual marriage flourish.

Companions are men who you find are better suited for friendship once you start dating.

Companions might want what you want when you want it, but perhaps you're not quite suitable for each other. I remember someone telling me right before I got serious about committing my singles walk to God that you "just know" when the man have been spending time with is the one. I agree partially. I don't think you "just know." I think the Holy Spirit and your own spirit of discernment will allow you to pick up on cues to let you know this man is suitable for you—and you for him. That's why, in later chapters I cover how to assess the men you're meeting so you know which one is suitable for you. I think you do (or should), however, start off knowing ultimately where you want to go in life. Then in time, it's easy for you to see whether or not you are a fit for each other.

So once you know who you are and where you're going (the first and second parts of the book are designed to help you uncover that), pay attention to how the men you're meeting fall into that plan—God's plan—for your life. If you feel in your heart that this man will make a really great friend, talk to him about that and keep the friendship that way unless the Holy Spirit reveals otherwise.

***Here are some tips to help you maintain a
pure and strong platonic friendship:***

1) **Don't flirt with him.** Flirting opens the door to
   romantically and sexually charge conversations. That
   in turn opens the door to sexually charged physical
   contact. You know where that goes.
2) **Don't kiss or engage in romantic physical
   contact.** It's the best way to ruin a strictly platonic
   friendship. It's also the best way to open the gateway
   to sex.
3) **Don't fantasize about him in sexual or
   romantic ways.** Your body will go where your mind
   takes it if you allow the fantasies to linger. If you
   fantasize about him sexually, you increase the chances
   of having sex with him when or if the opportunity
   presents itself.
4) **Don't spend large amounts of time together
   alone.** There's too much of a risk for you all to be
   spending hours at a time together alone. Even if you
   feel like you'd never be attracted to him romantically,
   that type of attraction could creep right up on you
   because you're comfortable around him and therefore
   not monitoring how much time alone you spend
   together.
5) **Don't have too many intimate conversations.**
   Intimacy is what helps associations and acquaintances
   blossom into deep, abiding friendships and
   relationships. But in platonic male-female
   friendships, you have to be diligent in watching what
   you share in conversations. Sharing deep secrets and
   hurts could make you emotionally dependent on him,
   which could lead to you wanting more than just
   friendship.

Gems in the Rough

Now, there's a fifth type of man that I didn't name in
the types of men you'll meet: a gem in the rough. I didn't
name this one because I really don't want you to focus on
him as the type of man you should date or court. There's
nothing wrong with a gem in the rough—after all, He's God's
child just like you. But remember that the beginning of a

godly marriage starts with two whole people. Gems in the rough often have issues that God needs to work out in them before they become suitable for marriage to the right woman. Most women are not spiritually attuned enough to God to be able to discern how God would want them to operate in a close, romantic relationship with someone who is an unbeliever or has walked away from the faith. So if you believe that a man you're dating is a gem in the rough, ask God to reveal how He wants you to proceed in that relationship.

I can say this because I used to be a gem in the rough. If I had met the man God had for me just a few years ago, we would have had a lot of unnecessary hardship and heartache if we had even gotten married. I thank God that He is a merciful father who doesn't always give out gifts before you're ready to receive them. Yes, God could have used the right man to help me along my life's path—but then again, I've accepted the fact that God knows what He's doing. I accept the fact that I could have scarred a good man if God had allowed that man to walk into my life before I was ready or able to handle that type of love and commitment. I also accept the fact that my own state of mind, heart, and spiritual condition could have kept me from recognizing the right man out of all the men I've met up to this point in my life.

And so it is with the gem in the rough. His state of mind, heart, and spiritual condition may not be conducive to allowing him to realize your worth as a marriage-worthy woman. Even though gems in the rough are good men deep inside, there's a lot of "coal" you'd have to chip away to get through to them. That's a job that only God can handle. Why? Because if you undertake it outside of God's will and without His protection, you'll most likely wind up hurt. Even if he does flourish and start to shine due to your love, time, and energy, you'll most likely wind up giving more than you ever intended to give and going farther than you ever expected to go. Ask a woman who has "dated" a man for years why she's still hanging on to him. It's most likely because she feels she's already invested so many years in him, and she doesn't want all the work she's put into him to benefit the next woman. We'll talk more about time and dating to courtship later on, but for now I just want you to get an understanding of why God needs to be the driving force between a relationship and eventual marriage between you and a gem in the rough.

Simply put, I believe you should be so in tune with God that you know for sure that you should be dating this type of man.

But even still, I like the gem in the rough. A good man's steps are ordered by the Lord. He may not believe like you believe, worship like you do, or know every nook of the Bible like you do. But if he has a heart for God or is at least willing to become closer to God, you might just have a winner on your hands. Even better, if he starts to show initiative in doing things like going to church, praying, and pursuing God on his own—without you encouraging him to do it—you're doing well. But if he's not a believer at all, don't go any further than friendship until there's a change. Bad company will corrupt good character unless you walk only within what God has ordained for that association.

Here's how you recognize a gem in the rough. He:

1) Respects you
2) Seeks to spend more time with you
3) May not have a strong relationship with God, but is willing to attend church and get to know God for himself after seeing your own relationship with Him
4) Is interested in you for who you are, not what you can do for him
5) Respects your values

So if you meet a gem in the rough...

The key here is to find out whether your basic life direction and goals, values, and attitudes match before you spend a significant amount of time together. The last thing you want to do is fall in love with a man who has no plans of strengthening his personal relationship with God, and who is a complete mismatch with you when it comes to values. To avoid this, make sure that you don't invest a lot of emotional or physical energy in the dating stage of interacting with this man. If you disregard that and let your emotions dictate your response to him, you'll be more likely to excuse differences in the basic areas you two need to have compatibility in.

Here are some examples of values so you'll get the idea:

Community involvement	Work ethic
Having/adopting children	Physical fitness
How to raise children your life	Living God's calling on
Living by biblical principles	Obeying God's instructions
Church attendance	Church involvement
Financial responsibility	

Chapter 13: Dating God's Way

So by now I hope you're wondering, "How exactly do we conduct ourselves during dating when the Bible really doesn't really talk about dating?" If so, I'm glad you asked.

First, I'm sure you've noticed that I use the phrase "dating God's way." It might seem like an oxymoron since you've noticed that the Bible doesn't talk about dating as we know it. So what I mean when I say dating God's way is that you honor God in dating. Because dating is something we've created in today's culture, you have to apply biblical principles to the process. We've already talked about what dating looks like according to popular culture versus dating based on biblical principles. But the main thing I want you to be able to do is to allow God's supernatural Holy Spirit and knowledge guide you through the process. That's the key that allows the dating and courtship processes to work the way God would want them to. So remember that successfully dating God's way requires you to maintain two things at all times: biblical dating and courtship know-how, and God's supernatural revelation.

To share those insights with you, I'm going to extract some key elements from the stories of Adam and Eve, Ruth and Boaz, and Rebekah and Jacob. In each of these stories, we'll cover how God's hand was on the men and women involved, the lifestyles and characteristics that they displayed, and implications you can apply to your own life to allow God to supernaturally guide the process.

Before I take you there, though, I want to clarify my stance on dating and courtship.

Dating – a non-sexual relationship between male and female friends that allows them to determine whether or not they should continue on into a courting relationship or remain friends.

Courting – a relationship between a man and a woman where it's been decided that you are or soon will be exclusive for the purpose of marriage in the near future. Sexual abstinence is still practiced until the wedding night or after.

The focus at this time is discovering each other on a deeper level and learning how to work, love, and live together.

In essence, dating is for collecting enough information to determine what type of relationship will be established between you and a man. Courting is an exclusive relationship where you and a man agree you are headed in the direction of marriage, and now you just need time together to solidify the journey towards marriage.

So basically, dating is something you can do as friends. With that, I think you can date more than one man at a time—but only if you stay in prayer and in submission to God. The minute you leave God's guidance, you make dating a sport. A sport where you try to find out how many men you can attract and even seduce. And that definitely is not God's best for you! If you only want to date one man at a time, that definitely works too.

The point, though, in dating is to determine "Okay, is this someone I should remain friends with? Or are we compatible and suited for marriage to each other? Or, is more time needed to determine in what way we should be in each other's lives? Or should we just break all ties now?" If you are preparing yourself for a husband, there really is no gray area here. Special precautions should be taken not to become emotionally, spiritually, or physically attached at all during dating. That means abstinence from sex and very limited or no time alone. It means focusing on developing a friendship, observing the man as you interact with him, and collecting information about him. Remember when we talked about not having sex outside of marriage? Well, believe it or not, pre-marital sex skews our judgment. And it seems to me that women are always the ones who are more negatively impacted by it. I hear from far more women than men saying, "He just stopped calling and coming by...and I gave him everything!" So to avoid this, just focus on developing the friendship, observing the man as you interact with him, and collecting information about him.

On the other hand we have courting. I believe that courting is what comes after dating, ***once you and a man***

you're dating mutually agree that you want to be exclusive and eventually marry. I got stuck on this for a while! I honestly thought you either dated or courted. But if you think about it—how are you going to come to the decision that you want to be in courtship with someone? Go out on a date! Several dates...many dates! Go on as many dates as you need to determine that you want to "take that person off the market." And that's what courting is in a nutshell. The man that's right for you is taking you off the market so he can marry you. Think of it this way: A man is going to court you because he sees that you are a good thing. He knows that if he doesn't court you, another man is going to see you, catch the fact that you're a good thing, and waste no time marrying you. And he doesn't want you to get away because he wants your undivided attention in the matters of love, so he can get to know you as you move towards marriage.

And keep this in mind... It does not take a man a long time to figure out that you're a wife and more specifically that you're his wife. Let me tell you...men are not like us. **They know about you without knowing you**. Most men know (sometimes within minutes of meeting you) whether you are a wife and whether it's highly likely that you're his wife. Timelines are different for everyone, so I'll just say this: As you abstain from sex outside of marriage, use the clarity that comes with it to discern whether or not a man is wasting your time, possibly using you to fill a void until someone else comes along, or if he's just not on the same page as you. The dating relationship is the perfect time to determine this.

So keeping these things in mind, first, let's start with Adam and Eve.

The starting point for Adam and Eve's story I want to use is when God brought the animals to Adam to name. Prior to this act, *God* noticed that there was no suitable match for Adam and said it wasn't good. I wonder if Adam even knew what was missing from his life. Or if he did, perhaps he couldn't quite articulate it to God. Either way, Adam was presented with a number of creatures—living creatures just like him—that were *not* suitable for him to marry. Then he put Adam into a deep sleep and created Eve—a woman made just for him.

From this story, I pulled out the following things I believe you should keep in mind to be successful in dating:

1) **Don't be "one of many."** Remember, Adam saw a lot of creatures before he saw Eve. Don't settle for being Mr. Maybe's one of many. We talked about how it can work out if you date more than one man at a time. But if the man you're seeing seems to be dating multiple women at the same time (including you), and you can tell that it's about some type of conquest, it's time to back off. The best-case scenario is that you'll "win the competition." The worst-case scenario, though, is that he'll hide it from you and all of a sudden will break up with you to get serious about someone else. Or, he could be honest about it, but if you really like him he knows you'll compete for his affections and time.

   If you can remain friends after giving him some space, that could be okay. But if you see that the friendship is not going to develop into anything more than that, leave it be. If a friendship does not develop and you see that you're just one of many women this man is playing games with, you should cut your losses and move on. If you push it, not only are you out of God's order, you're setting yourself up to be used and forgotten once Mr. Maybe decides to move on. You could also be setting yourself up to be used for convenience over a long period of time—time that you could be using to be free and available for the right man who wants you to be his one and only. This requires you to cultivate the mindset that you are worthy to be the only woman for the right man.

2) **Let God announce that you're the one.** I believe that God can speak to the right man regarding you. But even if God doesn't, remember that men know. In the story of Adam and Eve, it doesn't say that God told Adam exactly that Eve was the one for him. But

perhaps God placed an understanding in Adam that allowed him to see that Eve was the one for him. I also believe that He'll let you in on the conversation. Again, the Bible doesn't say Eve objected or that God said anything to her specifically. But after Adam claimed her, she became his wife. So perhaps God somehow let her in on what was going on, too. Don't be so anxious to move to the next level with this man you're dating that you "hear" God say that he's your husband or the one for you—when what you really heard was your own desires. God speaks to each of us in different ways and I know for sure that you can mistake his voice for your own heart's desires. To avoid that, just decide that you will allow God to speak to you about the man you are dating. Once you do that, He will show you the purpose of the man that is currently in your life.

Accept that God's "announcement" about the man in your life could just be the simple unfolding of events. Once you see this man's heart, mind, and spirit, it could just be clear that he's the one for you. Once we go through the ways to tell if he's the one for you, knowing will become easier for you!

3) **Let "Adam" say and demonstrate you're the one.** We don't know what all happened between Adam and Eve in the story of Eve's creation. What we do know is that Adam looked at Eve and said, "She is mine." Then, they were "married" before God. I put married in quotations because the Bible doesn't actually say they were married. But if you think about it, it sure looks a lot like they were married! Adam immediately recognized that Eve was the missing part of him—even though he was asleep when God took a part of his rib. He knew she wasn't like the rest of the animals he had named. So as soon as he saw her he said, "You're the one" and then he demonstrated this to be true by marrying her. Today, there will be a dating or courtship process before you get to marriage. So in between that initial contact and marriage, your guy will demonstrate by his actions

that you are the one for him. He'll ask for more of your time. You'll start to see that you're the only one he's spending a special type of time with. He'll start planning with you in mind. He might even demonstrate his plans for you before he says that you're the one. Either way he'll say and demonstrate and say, "Lady, you're *mine*"!

4) **Let God create you into the woman He wants you to be.** I believe that's what God was doing with Eve while Adam was asleep. He created her to be a perfect match for Adam. Now, today we are born and grow up as a whole person before we meet the right man. We aren't literally taken from our Adam's rib while he's asleep. But in a sense, there's still a process we go through in order to become the woman we need to be for that right man. And reflecting on the story of Adam and Eve, there's a sense that Adam knew when he saw her that she was the one who had been missing from his life. So continue to discover the woman God created you to be, continue pursuing your purpose, continue to be open to meeting, befriending, and dating men who may not be "your type." Continue to live with a sense of purpose, urgency, and joy. Because when you do, you stand a much better chance of being found by the man who has a "light bulb" moment once he sees and starts to pursue you.

5) **Let God work on Adam while He creates you**. I wondered if anything else besides the creation of Eve happened to Adam while he was asleep. Again, I don't know for sure. But what came to me after studying the passage of Eve's creation was that maybe God worked on Adam, too. Remember when I said I wondered if Adam even knew he was missing anything—even though God did? Well, the Bible doesn't say Adam knew. It says God knew it wasn't good for Adam to be alone. But Adam sure did know once he saw Eve that something had been missing—although he didn't even seem to be aware that she was missing before! So maybe God did some work on Adam to make him receptive to Eve.

As you continue on meeting and dating new men, remember that God has His hand on your Adam just like He has His hands on you. So while God works on you, He's working on your Adam. That's the perfect time to pray for him, think loving thoughts about him, and talk to God about him.

Now let's take a look at the story of Rebekah and Isaac (Genesis 24: 12-67)

1) **Develop a servant's heart.**
   Isaac's father sent their servant to find a wife for Isaac. The servant was given simple, but specific instructions. Rebekah—I think—made it easy for the servant to find her, because she was out and about serving. Better yet, she was doing the activity that lined up with what the servant was looking for. This made me wonder if being at the appointed place, at the appointed time, doing the appointed activity is a prerequisite to being found by the right man.

   > Based off their story, you can't go wrong with developing the heart of a servant. It's a sure fire way to be in the right place at the right time.

2) **Be willing to "go."** Rebekah was willing to relocate to be with Isaac. But this means something different for dating and courtship. In dating, be willing to go new places and try new things. Take your current friends up on their invitations. Go to parties and other social gatherings. Often, that's how you meet new people.

   > In courtship, be willing to relocate. If it's clear that you two are meant to be together, be willing to go wherever God is taking the both of you. Of course it's ideal that neither of you will have to uproot, but maintaining geographical roots is not worth losing out on marriage to a man who is just right for you.

3) **Be proactive and go the extra mile in service.**
The servant asked Rebekah for some water. But before he even came to where she was, she spotted him, and was prepared to assist him. And then she went above and beyond. She replenished his camels by giving them water as well—without him having to ask her to do so.

When you follow God's leading to give abundantly in service, you're not just allowing the right man to notice, you're developing the heart that's necessary to make a marriage work. Marriage is work; if you only want to do the bare minimum and you get agitated when asked to give even that, your marriage will be lukewarm at best. So as you practice in giving abundantly to others in service, you will become known as a woman with a heart for people and who would make a great wife.

4) **Be open to going out on blind dates.** This is similar to "be willing to go," and I came up with it because, in essence, Rebekah went on a blind date that led to marriage. She didn't know Isaac or the servant, and let's be honest—how many of us would go off with some strange man claiming to have a husband on the end of a journey to a foreign place? The last time I checked, that's how people come up missing!

So I don't want you to go off with strange people. I do, however, want you to be willing to go out on the blind dates that your friends set you up on. Especially if you're 30 and older, because this is the age where you have to be creative and open to safe options that you maybe didn't need to consider when you were in your teens and twenties. As long as you trust your friend's judgment and their knowledge of you, it can work out.

For some reason, it seems that both men and women are somewhat closed off to   the idea of going out on a blind date. Yet, more and more people are choosing to   sign up on dating websites. If I had to choose personally, I would rather go out on a blind date set up by a friend. I believe that my close friends know me well enough to know if a man they know would be a good match or not—even if it doesn't actually turn out that way. On the other hand, while I don't think online dating is the safest option, I think it can work if you go about it safely and smartly. I don't promote it, but always share tips on how to be safe if you're going to do it. I do, however, promote going on blind dates arranged by mutual friends.

Rebekah definitely was willing to go on a blind date! Once the servant told her that Isaac needed a wife, she went willingly. Although the intent was marriage, she agreed without seeing or meeting Isaac. So in a similar spirit, be open to your   friends' matchmaking efforts. They want to see you happy, single and on the road to marriage!

And finally, let's gain some insights from Ruth and Boaz (The Book of Ruth)

In summary, Ruth was the widowed daughter-in-law of Naomi, who was also a widow. Naomi's sons were married to Ruth and Orpah. After Naomi's husband and sons died, she had no choice but to return to her homeland. Orpah and Ruth originally planned to travel back with Naomi, but at Naomi's insistence, Orpah finally turned back and went home. Ruth refused and stayed by Naomi's side. One day, Ruth found one of Boaz's wheat fields, did some gleaning work, and met Boaz. Boaz extended kindness to her, showed interest in her, and eventually married her. So here are some lessons we can take from Ruth's story.

1) **Get a mentor.** I think Ruth might have missed the signals Boaz was giving her had it not been for Naomi. Granted, Naomi may have known Boaz well already since he was her distant relative. But Naomi represents that older woman who can provide an objective "bird's eye" view of a situation. So when Ruth came back with (literally) a bunch of wheat,

Naomi asked where she got it. Ruth told her about Boaz and that's when Naomi clued Ruth in to the cultural customs that led to marriage at that time.

See, Ruth was a foreigner in Naomi's hometown. But Ruth had a teachable spirit and was willing to do what she had to in order to take care of herself and her mother in law. Perhaps that's why Naomi wasted no time teaching her how to present herself to Boaz in the right way. Maybe Naomi knew Ruth would do what she told her to do, even if it didn't make sense to her. So you may be somewhat of a "foreigner" to the customs that actually lead to a godly marriage today. But you're in luck if you heed the insights in this book and find a godly mentor—a Naomi—who can teach you how to present yourself in a godly way to a man who is interested in you.

On another note, mentors are important because they help us to avoid giving up when we get frustrated or when we're falling out on the floor asking God, "Can I *please* get married before the rapture?" They often will assure you that at some point they felt the same way as you, or at least will sympathize with you. Then they can encourage you and give you godly, sound advice on how to move through that particular season of unrest, dissatisfaction, and doubt. They are living examples of who we want to become and are treasure chests filled with knowledge, strategy, and encouragement. Best of all, they set you up to be even better than they are!

2) **Embrace your purpose or calling wholeheartedly.** Ruth embraced her purpose wholeheartedly—which was to provide for herself and her mother-in-law. How do we know that? Because the foreman overseeing her only had a positive report about how hard she worked. She didn't let her destitute circumstance bankrupt her hope. She didn't let it stifle her ability to think creatively or problem-solve. Instead, she focused on the task at hand and didn't shy away from working in the grain fields.

I like to think that from hanging around Naomi, maybe she wanted to see God's hand move in a real way in her own life. This is all my imagination, but when I think about all that's not said in the book of Ruth, I think about a young woman who sat at her mother-in-law's feet long enough to learn about God, His power, and His ways. Maybe Naomi told her and Orpah (the other daughter-in-law that went back to Ruth's homeland) about God and was a living example of what God could do in a woman's life. Whatever it was, Ruth was determined to make it through her situation. She did it by wholeheartedly embracing her purpose for the moment. So whatever situation you're in now, think of ways where you can identify and fully embrace your purpose.

3) **Cultivate your reputation**. Ruth earned quite a positive reputation for herself. When Boaz noticed her out in the field and asked his foreman about her, the foreman had a good report. He said that she had been hard at work with few breaks. He could have complained that she was in the way, that she was lazy or had a bad attitude. But instead, he quickly reported her good qualities. I've learned that part of cultivating a positive reputation is being open to feedback from others—whether it's positive or not. In Ruth's case, Boaz had heard she was dedicated to her mother in law even though she really didn't have to be. But what about you? Do you know what those closest to you (whether close friends or casual acquaintances) think about you? I'm not asking you this to say you need to be overly concerned with or consumed by others' perceptions of you. But what other people think about you is important from the standpoint of how effective you are for God. Meaning, you could be the best evangelist ever, but if you have a tendency to be abrupt and direct, it could be experienced as cold and rude by the very people God has called you to serve. If you gain that reputation with a large number of people, it drastically diminishes the impact you can have for God because people generally don't want to

deal with ministers or Christians who are cold. So start by asking your closest friends what they think about you – both positive and negative – and ask God what you can do to improve the negative. Then cultivate your reputation in a way that diminishes the negative.

4) **Show appreciation for a man's kindness and generosity.** I don't believe women who say, "There are no good men out here." Just like I don't believe men who say, "There are no good women out here." They probably see them every day but overlook them because they don't come packaged the way they prefer. In fact, I'll bet you've overlooked many a small, but kind and chivalrous act towards you. And as a result, you probably didn't show any type of gratitude towards the man who displayed that kindness. So I want you to do something for me (better yet, this is for you!). I want you to make a habit of showing appreciation towards a man when he is kind, generous, and chivalrous. Smile and say, "Thank you so much." Tell him how kind he is. Give him a genuine compliment. Do anything you can to let him know that his act of kindness was noticed, received, and appreciated.

Naomi gave Ruth similar advice, although it was geared to specifically have Ruth indicate that she was interested in marriage to Boaz. But at the heart of her advice was having Ruth indicate that Boaz's kindness was noticed and received. This is important because most men will eventually move on if they don't receive any indication from you that you like them, that you appreciate them, or that you want to communicate or spend time together past just pleasantries in passing. So make sure that if you are interested in a man, that you show appreciation for his acts of kindness towards you.

5) **Respond affirmatively to a man's (nonsexual) advances.** This is similar to number 4, but now the stakes are higher. After you've given him the signal

that you have noticed his kindness towards you, his response might be asking you out on a date if he is interested in spending more time with you. Ruth accepted Boaz's invitation to eat at his table. It's just that simple, sis! If a man asks you out and you like him (or think you like him), go! If you're shy about doing this, it's a good thing for you that I'm not a matchmaker. You would probably love me, but hate to see me coming when you shied away from a perfectly good opportunity to go out on a fun date with a perfectly great guy. Again, God didn't birth the desire for marriage in my heart just for myself. He birthed it in my heart for you, too! And I know in my heart that God wants us to have love and get married according to His perfect plan. So when I tell you to respond affirmatively, I mean say yes. "Yes, I would love to go" or "I would love that" or "Thank you so much, yes I will go" or "What time and day are we going?" If you can't go out with him on the specific day and time he offers, say, "I would love to, but I can't then. Can we go on this time...?" Then offer an alternate time and day.

It's that simple. And remember this is the time to say yes. You don't know him and he doesn't know you. Even if you do know each other, chances are you didn't notice certain things about each other if you're just now going out on a first date. So now is the time to say yes because saying yes is necessary to find out what comes next. Remember that you're not committed to keep saying yes. You're only saying yes to finding out more about who he is and letting him find out more about you. So say yes, go, and have fun. And if you don't have fun...well, I know there will be more opportunities in the future to say yes.

So the other part of this that I have to address is saying no to a man's sexual advances. Again, the goal on this walk is abstinence from sex *outside* of marriage. If a man is making sexual advances towards you and he doesn't even know you or hasn't spent time with you, that's a major red flag. It means that he's pretty much only interested in figuring out the quickest way to get you to have sex with him. Sexual advances include invading your personal space, touching you in areas of your body that you know a friend or respectful man wouldn't touch, looking your body up and down, licking his lips or making sexual comments. The easiest way to deal with that is to say, "I'm abstaining from sex outside of marriage and you're making me uncomfortable." If he won't stop, leave and don't look back.

Remember that the goal in dating is to get to know the other person and have fun doing it. That's why you should avoid seeing each other alone in private residences or secluded places altogether— especially in the initial stage of your friendship where physical attraction is sometimes at its highest. So you want to choose activities that will promote conversation, bonding as friends, and teamwork, but inhibit the tendency to fall into sexual temptation.

Here are some safe activities for dates that will help you do that:

Golf	Ice skating
Miniature golf	Sports events
Rock climbing	Art gallery showings
Concerts	Open mic nights
Picnics	Having coffee or ice cream

Dinner after a movie: Make sure you pick something that will generate dialogue. The goal is to allow the both of you to better understand each other's beliefs.

What you're looking for in dating

So again, we said that dating is a non-sexual relationship between a man and a woman, where information is collected to determine the future status of the current relationship. Well, here are some specific things you need to look for in dating to help you determine whether or not you should stay friends, move on to courtship, or cut ties completely.

Leadership ability

In a godly marriage, your husband will be the head of your household. There are scriptures that support this, but my structure throughout this book regarding the family unit is based on Adam and Eve, since they were God's prototype for marriage. And God created Adam to be the leader of their marital unit. He gave Adam the assignment to be fruitful and multiply and then brought Eve to help him fulfill that assignment. Likewise, you will be "assigned" to your husband to help him fulfill the assignment that God has given him. Therefore, you want to assess leadership ability when you're dating. If a man has no goals in life, only follows his whims, and is not led by God, then don't continue dating him. Even if you do get married, you're going to be on one heck of an emotional roller coaster ride as he decides to swing from one thing to the other.

Decision-making ability

So if the man is the head of the household, that means decision-making will be part of his duty to his family. I want to assure you that it's not designed for him to make important decisions without you knowing. He also is not given that authority to abuse you and treat you like a slave. It's a tremendous responsibility that God holds him accountable for. That man will be accountable to God for you! It says in the Bible that God will hinder a man's prayer if he's not treating you right as his wife. But it's also clear in the Bible that God's design for marriage is for the man to take full responsibility for his family unit. So fully assess a man's decision-making ability. I'll let you in on a personal preference of mine: I would rather marry a man who makes a decision that turns out to be less than God's best for us, than to marry one who always leaves me in the position to make major decisions for our family. A man who will leave that responsibility to you all the time will also depend on you to fulfill other responsibilities of his, and then he might downplay *your* role in the family! Another thing you may want to consider is to choose a man who will value and use your input in the decision-making process. When it comes down to living the way God intended in a marriage, you want to choose someone who has the ability to make decisions and includes you in the decision-making process because he loves and values you.

Character

Honesty. Integrity. Faithfulness. These are examples of qualities that make up a person's character. And get this, by definition, character is "the way someone thinks, feels, and behaves: someone's personality" (m-w.com). And here I always thought that character was a specific set of qualities you either had or didn't have that qualified or disqualified you from certain jobs, communities, or stations of life. I think that's part of it. But as you can see, your character is made up of your thoughts, feelings, and behavior. So then I asked, "When it comes to marriage, what type of character do I need to have? What type of character should my husband have?"

Again, I went back to Adam and Eve. God gave Adam the assignment to be fruitful and multiply, and then gave him Eve to help him do that. So your character and that of the man you marry should allow you to be fruitful and multiply once you join in marriage. What does that mean? Your thoughts, feelings and behaviors should support the ongoing success of a life-long, healthy marriage. Here are some character traits, qualities, and abilities that would support that:

Commitment   Effective communication

Self-control   Patience   Honesty Generosity

Love   Integrity   Understanding   Compromise

Faithfulness   Loyalty

So you want to pay close attention to the character traits a man has. Take away his looks, talents, abilities, and personality traits, because at the end of the day, you're marrying a man's character. If you don't like his character, don't continue. Let God work on him and don't fall into the trap of believing you can change him.

Values and beliefs

A person's beliefs are what affects the very core of who they are and the type of life they live. The Bible tells us that, "For as he thinketh in his heart, so is he," which means that a person can tell you anything, but what matters is what they believe in their heart. Beliefs are so strong that they make you who you are—despite what you say or even what others say and believe about you. So you want to ask questions that reveal what his thoughts and beliefs are. If he does something you don't understand, don't be shy about asking what led him to do it. Once you understand his thought processes and beliefs, you'll have a very good understanding of how he sees life, God, himself, and you. Once you understand that, you'll also start to see what he values. If his beliefs and values don't match what's in the Word of God, don't continue dating him until you consult with God about it.

Temperament and personality

A lesson I've learned is that you have to take people as they are and allow God to decide whether or not to change them. Now, does that mean that you allow just anyone into your life or allow people to hurt you in any way? No. It does mean that you need to understand a person's make-up, disposition, and bent before you decide to have any type of long-term relationship. None of us are perfect. Just like someone has to decide whether or not they can accept your flaws in a long-term friendship or relationship, you have to do the same as well. So when you're dating, you want to consider how this man's temperament and personality are going to impact you. If you find that you have a low tolerance for every man you meet, it's time to figure out what's going on within you that's stirring up that intolerance. Remember to take into account whether or not each new man's temperament and personality complements your own. Don't try to figure out how you should change yourself or how you should change him. Consider what's been revealed and ask God to show you whether or not his temperament and personality are complementary to your own.

Personal relationship with God

I'm not going to say that you should dismiss a man who doesn't have a personal relationship with God. I personally know godly women who were pursued by men who had no personal relationship with God—and then got married. So God can send a man to you who doesn't have a relationship with Him. But those same women got married after that man got saved or recommitted to God, and was transformed by God. Those men already had character traits that would make them great husbands. The main thing they were missing was a personal relationship with God. So if you meet a man who doesn't have a personal relationship with God, proceed with caution. Consult with God every step of the way and allow your own example of close fellowship with God to make him want more of God.

If the man you meet does have a personal relationship with God, observe it by the fruit of the Spirit in his life. Keep this verse in mind: "But the Holy Spirit produces this kind of fruit in our lives: love, joy, peace, patience, kindness, goodness, faithfulness, [23] gentleness, and self-control. There is no law against these things!" If a man claims to have a relationship with God but he's not producing this type of fruit in his life, steer clear. Likewise, you should be producing this type of fruit in your life as you grow in your relationship with God.

And be open to learning something new from him if you do see this fruit in his life. He might have a deeper and stronger walk than you. So find out the areas you both are strong and weak in, and how you can use your strengths complement each other.

Compatibility

Does this person have habits you can't live with, let alone tolerate for more than five minutes? Do they respect you? Do you respect them? Do you feel like you understand each other or like you're from two different planets? Simply put, compatibility is your ability to work with, live with, and do life with another person despite differences of opinion, background, or even beliefs. It can usually be cultivated, provided that you both have the same general goal or vision for life. It's not exactly about liking a man, although there's nothing wrong with wanting to be in a marriage where you like each other. After all, this is someone you're vowing to spend the rest of your life with! But more than that, you want to see that you can simply be around him, feel understood by him, understand him, and have a sense that you are on the same page when it comes to the direction of your life together.

"Can two people walk together without agreeing on the direction?" (Amos 3:3, NLT). The fruit of agreement is important amidst life difficulties, discussions, and having a place of refuge when life gets hard. Have you ever had a friend who you just wanted to be around when your life felt unstable? They were calm and no matter what you talked about, you always seemed to come to an agreement despite differing opinions? Well, with your husband, you should be able to walk together for a lifetime because you agree on the Word of God and you agree in the areas of life that impact the success of having a lifelong, godly marriage. The opposite of agreement is strife, discord, and bickering. No matter what, you can't come to an agreement on anything because no one wants to give up their own way. Any man who creates this type of atmosphere in a relationship is not the right man for you.

Emotional, spiritual, and physical compatibility are important as well. If you're emotionally healthy but he can't control his anger or always seems to be up and down with mood swings, and it negatively impacts you, you're not emotionally compatible. Likewise, if one of you still needs to heal from your last relationship while the other is ready for true love in a godly marriage, you're not compatible. Spiritually, you want someone who at least agrees that life should be an ongoing commitment to growing in your walk with God, even if one of you has significantly more spiritual and emotional maturity than the other. If you find that there is a significant gap in emotional and spiritual maturity, don't continue dating unless you consult God about it.

And last is physical compatibility. Since, by God's standard, you abstain from sex outside of marriage, you want pay attention to whether or not you are attracted to the man you feel may be right for you. Avoid fantasizing about getting physical with him, but make note of if you feel chemistry when you're with him. It doesn't have to just be a physical attraction. Maybe you love his personality, his sense of humor, or just the way he treats you and people in general. Maybe you love that no matter what, he's so positive and encouraging. And yes, it is okay to like the way he looks! When God gives you an attraction to another person, it's not about being consumed with impatience over when you can get your hands on him. It's about a true enjoyment of that other person, while taking into account everything about them—even their flaws.

Whatever you do...

Make sure that you communicate with the men you meet. As you go about your daily life, incorporating the ground we've covered on how to be the best you inside and out, allow the Holy Spirit to guide you in what you share and when. Whatever you do, make sure that you communicate your standards and beliefs up front. Be kind, but firm. Leave the pride out of "doing this God's way." No matter what, you want to represent God's love even if the two of you move on.

When you communicate your standard, be prepared for what comes next. The right man will stay. The ones who are only interested in you for selfish reasons will not. Here are two scriptures that I meditated on when I first committed to abstinence before marriage to help me deal with the disappointment of having yet another man walk away after disclosing my stance:

"These people left our churches, but they never really belonged with us; otherwise they would have

stayed with us. When they left, it proved that they did not belong with us." 1 John 2:19, KJV

If he's the man for you, he will stay after you prove that you're living your life by God's standards. It's just that simple. Now, I know sometimes God can move in ways that we don't understand and as a result we might wind up separated from someone who is actually a great match for us. Then we meet up at a later time and things happen just as quickly as they should (remember, it can take as little as a few months for the right man to commit to you). But generally, if a man wants to have you in his life, he will quickly and clearly make the necessary steps to keep you. That's why clearly communicating that you're living your life by God's standards is a win for you. It allows you to see early on whether he's someone who is meant for you. But you have to live by God's standards! Let that man be convicted by your actions...

"Guard your heart above all else, for it determines the course of your life." Proverbs 4:23, NLT

I realized shortly after my encounter with God that night in Isaiah 30 that one of the most valuable inner resources I had in terms of being attractive to a man was my energy. When you allow yourself to daydream about men you know very little about just because you think they may be "the one," you find yourself devastated once you clearly see that he is not. Now, imagine doing that over and over...and over again. And having sex will only make it worse. After a while, it wears your spirit down and pollutes your heart. So you have to be careful to monitor your thoughts about the men you meet. Take things as they come when you interact. Don't overanalyze what he says and does. And don't fantasize about what your first name and his last name look like together. Value your purity of heart and the preservation of your energy over constantly wondering if this new man is the one.

Chapter 14: How Will I Know If He's the Right One?

I'm writing this chapter because I do believe there is a way to know if a man that you've met since you've started this journey is right for you. Women I've talked to who are happily married said they "just knew." But I continued to talk to them until they explained how they "just knew."

I touched on what to look for in dating, and the next chapter will cover how to create a good list of desired traits in the man you want to marry, so that you'll know he's the one for you. So for now, I want to share what finding my current church home taught me about knowing the man you're dating is the right one for you. Here's my testimony:

I believe the first time I attended New Life Providence was some time in August 2013. I had only visited a few other churches, but I really didn't have the energy or interest in visiting church after church. In fact, before I left Djibouti, Africa, in July of 2013, I had talked to God about finding a church home. I confessed something like this to Him: "God, I'm tired of going to churches where the pastors and worship leaders bully you into participating in particular worship styles or responses to the preacher's message. And I don't know why—but I really want to go to a multi-cultural church. I want to worship with all kinds of people. And God, is it even possible to go to a church that has social events where people meet and actually get to know each other?"

I had come to a point in my walk where I knew I needed a church home and that it was not something peripheral to my life. I felt the need to make my church home a central, permanent part of my life. I knew the experiences I'd had in church up to that point in my life were the main reasons I didn't reach out to people in the church more and as a result I only knew people there in passing. I was tired of having shallow relationships in the one place in my life where deep, abiding relationships should be flourishing. I was ready for something new. I was willing to let go of church as I knew it to get something new from God.

Well, my mother visited me Hampton Roads, Virginia from July to October of that year. We hadn't spent very much time together face to face in a while because I had lived in Japan for three years, then in Africa for a year. She knew I wanted to find a church home, and she wanted to attend an AME church while she was there. She found an AME church one week that was right down the street from the Chesapeake campus of New Life. She agreed to go with me to New Life one Sunday, then we would go to the AME church the following Sunday. The Saturday before we were supposed to go to New Life, I was driving home from the store and Hezekiah's song "Every Praise" came on. I love that song, and asked God: "Lord, I know I haven't even been to this church, but if it's the right church for me, please let the choir sing this song!"

We walked in after praise and worship had already started and the next song they sang was "Every Praise"! I felt so overwhelmed that I cried. I had felt God's spirit the minute I walked through the door and although I never really believed in God giving you a sign before, I was sure that day that He could.

To make a long story short, I didn't go to the AME church the following Sunday. I kept going to New Life Providence. This church is a large church, so they have what we call "life groups" where you meet with people weekly or once a month based on common interests. I started attending a life group for young women the following month and made some beautiful connections there with the other women. At some point I also started participating in the single's monthly ministry and the women's prayer group every Sunday. And I'm still amazed at the examples the women in this ministry provide.

In February of 2014, I knew it was time to join. The first Sunday after New Year's Eve service, Pastor Dan made the offer for those of us who had been attending regularly, but still hadn't joined, to consider joining. What sold me was when he said, "Joining a church and just attending every now and then is like the difference between just casually dating and decided to make the commitment that leads to marriage. At some point, you have to decide if you're committed or not." So after only six months of attending I made the decision to become a member, and my life has been better for that decision.

So here are the lessons I learned from this:

You and your future husband will complement each other in areas that have bearing on a godly marriage.

Although I think we should know what we need and want in a husband, I think our "list" can be off-center. Meaning, "the list" that your friends and even well-meaning fellow Christians tell you to make are often made up of surface qualities that have no bearing on a godly marriage. We'll go over how to build the right type of list in a later chapter.

But what my church home taught me was that you should know what you need (per the Word of God, which we just covered) to sustain a godly marriage, and what you desire. Going to a multi-cultural church was simply a desire I had. I didn't know why I wanted that type of church home, but I did know that I had a deep need to be rooted in the Word of God and I wanted a church home that would help me do that. I knew I was in a different season and was open to whatever that meant. Looking back, I suspect God may have put the desire there so I would be open to New Life once I discovered it—since it was so different from what I had experienced at other churches. If I had dismissed New Life on the basis that it was multicultural, I could have missed out on all the spiritual growth I've gained as a result of being a member.

So in dating to courtship, that could look like you being open to dating a man who is outside of your race because you're open to whomever is the right man for you. You don't *require* a man to be outside of your race, but you're open to it.

The desire to go to the next level will be communicated

Had Pastor Dan not said, "Joining a church home is similar to going from dating to marriage. At some point, you have to walk away or make the commitment" I may have taken a lot longer to decide. I also may not have gotten the feeling that I was in the right church home. I didn't feel pressured at all to join when he said that. But his clear communication about the desire for those who were un-churched but faithful in attendance to join was what I needed to realize that New Life was the church home for me. I could have declined, but the benefits of joining were clear based on what I'd already seen. I knew I would have been missing out!

Women often ask, "How will I know if he's the one for me?" And the truth is that he will tell you he wants to marry you, and then he will marry you. Just like Adam saw Eve and then married her. As the Spirit of God is invisible, we can still see Him. How? Because He bears His fruit in our lives. Likewise, the man who's right for you will verbally communicate his desire to court and then marry you. You always have the choice to say no. But if he's the one for you, I guarantee that you won't!

All information you need to make a decision will come to light

Although I believe in my heart that God showed me a sign on the first visit that New Life was the church home for me, I needed more information. I talked to God about my reservations and I truly believe that as a result, God showed me the information I needed to make an informed decision.

Likewise, when a man is the right one for you, all the information you need will be revealed. But you have to pay attention and not be distracted. In order to do that, you have to remain objective and fight falling in love too early. Because once you do, you tend to overlook or ignore red flags. So while you maintain your objectivity, remember to pay attention to the information that this man is revealing about himself. Pay attention to what others say about him— in front of him or when he's absent. Watch the way he interacts with others.

It doesn't take long

I joined my church within six months of attending. In fact, I'd already become active in the smaller groups and made connections with people there prior to joining. I knew it was the right church for me, but in the back of my mind I still wondered if I should join. Even with the doubt, it still didn't take long. In fact, the only reason I didn't join sooner was because I was out of town during the first opportunity to join!

A man who wants you as his wife will not take years to decide he wants to marry you or even talk about planning for the future. Any man you're dating who says that he needs to live with you first or just wants to see how things go is not serious about you. He's only serious about getting what he needs from you on his terms. I want to be clear here. Any man who will date you for years at a time without exclusivity or commitment is wasting your time. He's wasting your time because now you're focused on how to keep him happy and how to get him to commit to you, when you could be focusing on how to live fully as a single and becoming whole, so that the right man will take notice and marry you. So if you're currently involved with a man, you've been on and off for years, or you've been committed to him without any real commitment from him, it's time to let go. I'm not saying it couldn't work out later, but for now, you need to work on committing to God, His standards, and living a full life free from ungodly soul ties.

With the right man, the only thing that will take years at a time is building a marriage and life together. Ladies, it just does not take years to get married unless there's clear guidance from God that you two should have a longer courtship and engagement. I personally know couples who dated and courted God's way in a matter of just months before they knew marriage was on the horizon. The time it takes to actually make it to the altar depends on you and your husband to be. But it does not take years. If a new man you're dating requests more of your time after a few months, but he's not indicating marriage in his actions or verbal communication, pull back to just friendship until you know what his intentions are. Don't *ever* give a man husband privileges without the commitment of marriage. Only give more of your time, attention, and love to a man who has clearly indicated that he wants to move from just dating to courtship, then marriage.

The courtship time will just be confirmation of what you already knew.

I used to wonder why, if you knew God put you together, does it still take "so long" to get married. Well, God answered me and said, "I didn't make the earth in one day." Let me tell you, if you don't already have a good or close relationship with God, keep working on it, because His answers to life's dilemmas and puzzles will amaze you. But I've digressed. God didn't make the earth in a day. He didn't reveal to me what all He was doing outside of what was documented in Genesis in regards to the formation of the earth. But I knew what He meant is that it takes time to forge a lasting relationship even when you know it's God-ordained. Although the agreement to marry can and will happen relatively quickly, you still need that time to let the relationship unfold and enjoy it.

The same thing happened when I started attending my church. Although I sensed it was the church for me in the first visit, I still needed to see that it was. I needed to see that they had the fellowship I needed. I needed to see that they had opportunities for me to be involved in the community outside of church. I needed to see that the members were loving and that they wanted to be in fellowship with other believers as well. If I had taken the plunge to join without knowing my church's pros and cons, I would have felt fooled or shortchanged. But now that I know what my church does well and what it's working to improve on, I feel that I've made an informed decision in joining a church that isn't perfect, but that's perfect for me.

Chapter 15: The Infamous "Dream Man" List: How to Know What You Need and Want in a Husband

"And then GOD answered: "Write this. Write what you see. Write it out in big block letters so that it can be read on the run."

Habakkuk 2:2, The Message

"Have you made a list of what you want in a husband?" was the recurring question I've either been asked or seen asked of other single women.

First, let me say that I don't have a problem with making a list. I think it's actually a great exercise because it allows you to discover what you desire, what's important, and what is not. Writing things down is a godly principle (Habakkak 2:2). What's ungodly is listing things that have no bearing on a godly marriage.

For instance, writing down "has to have a six-pack" has no bearing on a godly marriage. But I think it's godly to desire a husband who "is physically active and healthy." God says our body is a temple and one of the ways we care for it is by working out.

To give you a little more perspective on where I'm coming from, I want to take you to the part of David's story when the prophet Samuel was looking for a king to replace Saul—which was David. God told Him where to go and even who to talk to (Jesse, David's father), but didn't fill him in on who, exactly, he was looking for. What's so amazing to me is that Samuel had his own version of the list. Want to know how I know? He took one look at David's brother Eliab and just *knew* he was one! But God corrected him and reminded him that what was on the inside was going to qualify His choice as the next king of Israel.

To make a long story short, when David is presented to Samuel, the Word tells us:

"So Jesse sent for him. He was dark and handsome, with beautiful eyes. And the LORD said, "This is the one; anoint him.""

1 Samuel 16: 12, NLT

I chose the NLT translation because this version always speaks to my spirit. And it is the basis of this exercise of creating the list. What I want you to consider is that although David was considered the runt of the litter by his father, and Samuel thought Eliab looked the part of a king, God said that David was dark and handsome, had beautiful eyes, and was the chosen one. Could it be, my dear sisters in Christ, that once we tune into what God says about the men He brings in front of us, we tap into the power He's given us as women to see a man's heart and inner being? And *then*, his natural qualities become attractive?

With this thought in mind, let's discover a new way to build those lists so we can leave room for God to reveal to us the good and right choice for a husband.

Let's go back over the areas I told you to look for in dating, and to observe in courtship. I want you to write the answers down in the space I provide.

Character:

Again, your character is your thoughts, beliefs, emotions, and behaviors. It's the core of who you are. Character is the pillar of a lifelong, healthy, godly marriage. You and your husband have to have characters that will support this. It's like building a house or another facility. If the foundation is weak or corrupted, eventually the house will come down. If it doesn't come down, be prepared to withstand difficult living conditions.

Personality is similar, but think of it as the outward extension of who you are. For instance, you can believe that God is loving, and that loving others is a worthwhile way to spend your life. As a result, your personality—whether you're extroverted or introverted—will be friendly towards others. You may not be a big talker, but your words towards others will be kind and encouraging. So you have a friendly personality.

Habits are also somewhat of an extension of a person's character. Compulsive habits like smoking and consuming too much alcohol, caffeine, and certain foods often signal a weakness in character. Likewise, certain mannerisms, like rolling your eyes at people every time they say or do something you don't like, are a result of a person's thought processes that have ingrained over time. It signals hostility towards others and sometimes a defeatist attitude.

So let's take some time now to assess your character and to discover what character traits your future husband should have (and those that you would want him to have).

1) What are your values or what do you value in life? (i.e., community service, generosity, kindness, Christ-centered living, etc.)

_____

_____

_____

_____

2) What values do you want your husband to have?

_____

_____

_____

_____

3) What do you believe: about yourself, about others, about God, about life? Are they consistent with beliefs that would support a lifelong, healthy, godly marriage?

_____

_____

_____

_____

_____

4) What beliefs do you think your husband should have?

_____

_____

_____

_____

5) What are some character flaws you believe you couldn't live with?

_____

_____

_____

_____

6) What character flaws do you recognize in yourself?

_____

_____

_____

_____

7) Habits are an outward sign of character and personality traits. What habits are you unwilling to live with? (I.e., smoking, heavy drinking, etc.)

_____

_____

_____

_____

8) What habits do you have that are counterproductive and destructive?

_____

_____

_____

_____

And here's a special part of character that you also want to consider. How he treats others:

> How does he treat people who serve for a living (janitors, waiters/waitresses, store clerks, etc.)?
> How do you treat them?
> How does he treat people who can't do anything for him?
> How do you treat them?
> How does he treat his children from previous relationships (if he has any)?
> How does he treat strangers? Friends? Family? Coworkers?

Personality/temperament:

1) What personality traits appeal to you in a man and why? (I.e., laidback, upbeat, driven, etc.)

_____

_____

_____

_____

2) What is your own personality and temperament?

_____

_____

_____

_____

3) What personality traits of your own have you gotten the most compliments on? How about the most complaints?

_____

_____

_____

_____

4) What personality traits in others do you feel you can't stand?

_____

_____

_____

_____

5) What do you want to achieve together with your husband? (I.e., raising godly children, co-partnering a ministry, owning a home, etc.)

_____

_____

_____

_____

6) What is your temperament? (Moody, fiery, stoic, dramatic, etc.)

_____

_____

_____

_____

7) What type of temperament would complement your own?

_____

_____

_____

_____

Leadership ability

First, I want to re-emphasize that a man's leadership in your life is not the same as him dominating and abusing you. And abusing you could simply mean that he denies you of your role in the marriage—to influence him and the decision-making process. So when assessing a man's leadership ability, you're not just assessing how he directs the two of you as a team or unit, you're assessing his ability to allow you to have a voice and say in the affairs of your life together. True leaders—and I know this from experience—don't dictate. They ensure that good order is established and maintained. They don't rely only on their own personal doctrine of truth. They know what they know, but most often will include and depend on the input and say-so from the members of their supporting team.

Another test of a good leader is to look at who they follow. You can't really be an effective leader without being submitted to God's authority and the authority of those he places over you.

Third, good leaders know when to call for help. They know they can't do everything alone. They also know that they make mistakes and that it's better to admit them and ask for assistance to recover if necessary.

So here are some questions to ask him to assess his ability to lead—as it pertains to a marriage and family.

1) Who are your mentors?
2) Have you ever had a leadership position before? What was that experience like for you?
3) What type of relationship did your mother and father have?
4) What do you feel the man's role is in a marriage? (This is key. Although the man's place is at the head of the family unit, God never intended for it to be an opportunity to demean and degrade the wife.)
5) Are you currently submitted to older men's authority or leadership?
6) Would you be open to pre-marital counseling?
7) Would you attend counseling for marital problems?
8) What was your relationship like with your father?
9) What was your relationship like with your mother?
10) What were your past relationships with authority figures like (i.e., teachers, principals, coaches, parents, bosses, law enforcement, etc.)

Now it's time to consider your experience with leadership. Answer these following questions:

1) Have you ever held any leadership positions? When and what was the outcome of your leadership?

_____

_____

_____

_____

2) What's your response to leadership? (I.e., rebel, submit, question, undermine, etc.)

3) _____

_____

_____

_____

4) Do you often find yourself leading or following in your social circles?

_____

_____

_____

_____

5) How would you describe your own relationship with people who were authorities in the past: teachers, principals, parents, law enforcement, coaches, bosses, etc.?

_____

_____

_____

_____

_____

_____

_____

_____

_____

Decision-making ability

Point blank. Can the man you're dating make a decision and stick to it? If he can't, don't be surprised if you actually do get married, and he relies on you to make decisions for certain things and then eventually everything. That's out of order since God created Eve as the helper to Adam—who was given the task and responsibility that goes along with it.

So you want to assess two things: *can* he make effective decisions, and *how* does he make those decisions. If he can't make decisions effectively, is always "saddling the fence," or constantly second-guesses himself, consult with God before you continue dating. Likewise, if he's controlling in his decision-making process, only considers his point of view, and never asks for input when he's making a decision that affects others, you also want to consult with God before you proceed in dating. So to assess...

Here are a few words to help you see how he makes his decisions:

Quick	Slow	Deliberate
Reckless	Authoritarian	Inclusive
Authoritative	Collective	

Values and beliefs

I heard someone say that you can judge what a person values by what they spend their money and time on. I think they definitely had a point. Likewise, I think you can also observe a person's character and get an idea of what they believe by what they say (repeatedly or only a few times). So here are a few things to consider when figuring out what his values and beliefs are:

1) What does he seem to spend a significant amount of his money and time on?
2) Are they things you would spend significant amounts of money and time on?
3) If not, how do you feel about being in a lifelong, committed marriage to someone who spends significant amounts of money and time on those things?
4) What does he say about himself? Others? God? His family? His friends? His job? Life?
5) Have these things made you uncomfortable?

Now, don't forget to observe the same things regarding yourself!

Compatibility

Compatibility is the glue that will help you stay with your husband in a lifelong marriage. Amos 3:3 epitomizes compatibility: "Can two people walk together without agreeing on the direction?" If you can't agree on the key areas of how you want to live your life, you're incompatible. You can have a strong physical attraction. You can even like each other a lot. You can be as in love as two people can be. But if you're incompatible and can't compromise, you'll be lining up for divorce court. And according to the Word of God, incompatibility isn't grounds for divorce. Which means you shouldn't get married if you're incompatible.

So, look at your current relationships and consider the following.

1) Who do you get along with best? What character and personality traits do they have?

_____

_____

_____

_____

_____

_____

_____

_____

2) Who can you not get along with no matter how hard you try? What character and personality traits do they have?

_____

_____

_____

_____

3) Now think about having a lifelong commitment to your husband. What character and personality traits do you want them to have?

_____

_____

_____

_____

_____

_____

_____

_____

4) What qualities would you want your husband to have that you believe would help you two get along, agree and have a lifelong marriage?

_____

_____

_____

_____

5) Think again about having a lifelong commitment to your husband. What character and personality traits would he have that you believe would undermine a healthy, lifelong marriage?

_____

_____

_____

_____

6) And last, but most importantly, assess yourself. What character and personality traits do you believe you have that would support a healthy, lifelong marriage?

What personality and character traits have acquaintances and close friends said you have that make it easy for them to get along with you? (If you're not sure, ask your trusted friends and close family members.)

_____

_____

_____

_____

Personal relationship with God

Let's go back over the fruits of the Spirit: "But the Holy Spirit produces this kind of fruit in our lives: love, joy, peace, patience, kindness, goodness, faithfulness, gentleness, and self-control. There is no law against these things!" (Galatians 5:22-23, NTL).

Although some of these can be considered character traits, in general, this is how you can measure a man's (and your own) personal relationship with God. The fruit of the Spirit is a natural byproduct of a growing relationship with God.

1) In the men you've dated, how many of these characteristics have they had?

_____

_____

_____

_____

2) How many of these characteristics do you have?

_____

_____

_____

_____

_____

_____

_____

_____

3) Which characteristics do you believe you need to work on?

_____

_____

_____

_____

4) With any man you're dating now, how many of these characteristics do they have?

_____

_____

_____

_____

_____

_____

_____

Use this area for men you date in the future:

_____

_____

_____

_____

_____

_____

_____

_____

Now that you've answered these questions, I'll explain what we're doing with the answers. Notice that none of them talked about what your dream husband looks like, the type of job he has, or how much money he makes. They don't encourage you to list very many external qualities—except for personality and habits. That's because the goal is to focus first on assessing a man by his inner qualities that have bearing on a godly marriage. These are the most important because at the end of the day, no matter how sexually compatible you are, or how much you're in love, those inward qualities can eventually bankrupt your marriage if you're mismatched.

Once you see the inner qualities that are a match for you, then you can focus on discovering your desires from the standpoint of preparing for a godly marriage. God knows you want things like being attracted to your husband, being physically pleased and pleasing to him, and being cared for financially and materially. And if you trust Him, I believe He'll grant those desires because they are good things. But we have to get to the root of what holds a marriage together.

Now review your answers in the questions you just completed, pull out words that you've listed frequently or that summarize what it seems you need, then list them all separately in the left column below. Next to each word, find a scripture that supports it.

I need: The scripture that supports this
is:

_____   _____

_____   _____

_____   _____

_____   _____

_____   _____

_____   _____

_____   _____

_____   _____

_____   _____

_____   _____

_____   _____

_____   _____

If your list is longer, that's okay. You can use your personal notebook or journal and keep going.

So...how did you do? Did you find a scripture that supported each thing you want? If not, here are a few things to do:

1) Keep reading and studying the Word. It took time for me to read it and understand what I was reading. So if

you don't find it right away, it could just be that you're not familiar yet with the Word. Keep at it!

2) If after months of study you still can't find it, it's time to pray about it. In your prayer time ask God to reveal the motive in your heart for this desire. Not all solutions in life are expressly stated in the Bible. That's why I do what I do, and I believe it's why many inspirational authors, ministers, and business people do what they do—to share what they've learned about living a godly life. So take this opportunity to discover what God could be teaching you about your own desires.

And of course, you can always revise your list. If you get stuck or have questions, e-mail me at afi@authoroffaithmin.com!

The Executive Decisions I Made to Be Open to and Ready for Love and Marriage

If you're going to live your life God's way, you're going to have to make some executive decisions. In my life, I remember every time I made an executive decision. An executive decision is one you make, don't waiver from and deal with the consequences if you're wrong. It's standing in the confidence that you made a decision, not necessarily that it was the right one. It's not backing down from your determination to get to where you know or believe God is calling you, despite how things look now.

The beauty about having a relationship with God is that he will override those executive decisions if He knows that even though you're making them according to your best ability, that they will lead you down the wrong path. That's why by the time I decided I did want to marry and have a family, I knew God would tell me if it just wasn't in His life plan for me. Everyone is different. We are all unique and it's a scientific fact that even if you have an identical twin, there will never be another you. So I want you to consider what I'm about to say in two ways.

In order to have the husband God wants for you, *you* have to make some decisions.

Now, first, consider all we've discussed in the book already and think about what decisions you individually need to make. Second, consider the personal decisions I made in my own life—but use them only as a guideline or *inspiration* for your own executive decisions.

In order to receive the husband I believe God has for me, I decided that...

1) I will *not* be envious about someone else's marriage.

I did this because I never understood why it seemed like women who never even wanted to be married in the first place were *already married*! Yet, here I was—desiring marriage—and still single. First of all, you don't know that person's situation. Second of all, being green with envy is not attractive. If you're saying "I'm not envious!" but you're constantly wondering why it was so easy for "so-and-so" to get married when you're more attractive, have a better personality, or whatever else—you are envious! And you're telling God that what He's done in your life isn't good enough. So until you can let that go, you can't leave room for God to bless you with what He has for you.

2) I will not become anxious about being single past 30.

I didn't even decide I wanted to be married for sure until I was in my late 20s! But sometimes we look at movies or people we know in real life and wonder why we don't have what they do—for example, marriage and children—by a certain age. It's almost as if we forget that our life path can be completely different from theirs. But singleness in your 30s can be hard when you're looking at people who have already had what you want for already—especially if they're younger than you. It makes you feel like you're an outsider and that God has forgotten about you. I have a right to feel how I feel and so you do, but at the end of the day, we don't have to let the anxiety that comes with working through those emotions consume me and derail the rest of our life.

3) I will not question feeling convicted about God's standards.

There were two standards that I felt convicted by over time: abstaining from sex outside of marriage and being alone with a man I was dating or building a friendship with. In the back of my mind there was the nagging question "But if I 'go all in' with God's standards, how am I ever going to meet a guy and get married?" Well, one day I finally came to grips with the fact that living for God just might mean that I might not get the desire of my heart. Which leads me to the next decision.

4) I will uphold God's standards no matter what.

At the end of the day, God is the one who will never leave or forsake us. Yet how many times do we forego His standards to hold on to someone who never intended to stay? Doing this is like getting out of a long wait line to hop in one that's much shorter, only to find out the customer service rep can't help you. Then by the time you get back in the first line, it's twice the length and now you have to wait twice as long as you would have if you had just stayed where you were.

When we crawl back to God after disobeying and storming off to have our own way, we ultimately wind up hurting ourselves. God hurts for us and it hurts Him that you've walked away. But looking to a man to fill what he cannot hurts you much more than it hurts God.

5) I will allow the Holy Spirit to guide my interactions during dating and courtship.

Although I'm an introvert, I've never had a problem doing what I intended to do. I'm strong-willed like that! So it was hard for me to learn how to let God lead me, and to let the Holy Spirit whisper which way to go each day. Not because I just wanted to rebel, but it's just who I am.

But now, I've applied that strong will to following God as best as I can. The truth is that some good things came of following my own will, and some bad things did as well. And part of God helping me grow was allowing me to see that His ways are always better—that my own reasoning is no match for the Holy Spirit's intelligence.

6) I will believe that I am valuable because Jesus Christ died to save my soul.

Like many women, I struggled with my self-esteem as a girl. It carried over into my young adulthood, but God healed me and helped me to see that I was valuable (as we all are) simply because He loved me. My understanding of what Christ really did on the cross was what helped me to see that. No one dies a death like that for others unless they really love them. We are loved deeply by God. "And may you have the power to understand, as all God's people should, how wide, how long, how high, and how deep his love is" (Ephesians 3:18, NLT).

7) I will allow God to reveal to me what I need in a husband.

Again, God's ways are better than ours. He knows better than you do what you need in a husband. Remember what it says in Matthew 6:8 (NLT): "Do not be like them, for your Father knows what you need before you ask him." Therefore, it only makes sense.

8) I will live my life to the fullest.

This is important, because if you're not careful, you'll find yourself literally waiting for a man to show up in your life before you start living it. Here's that that looks like: you'll wait to travel to certain places, further your education, buy a house, pursue a certain career, or any of your other desires. It's understandable that you want to share certain things in your life with the right person. But it's just as good to have lived a good life at the point when you meet the right man as it is to meet him before you live many of your dreams.

9) I will not fall into desperation.

I think we fall into the trap of desperation because we believe God doesn't care what we're going through, and because we allow ourselves to covet what someone else has when we believe it's what we want. So we stop asking God for the desires of our hearts and take matters into our own hands out of desperation. I avoid that trap by meditating on this: "So if you sinful people know how to give good gifts to your children, how much more will your heavenly Father give good gifts to those who ask him" (Matthew 7:11, NLT).

10) I will not intentionally put myself in situations where I compromise what God is trying to do in my life.

"Run from sexual sin! No other sin so clearly affects the body as this one does. For sexual immorality is a sin against your own body" (1 Corinthians 6:18 NLT). Running from and avoiding sexual sin is the only way to avoid falling into sexual sin. So by putting yourself in situations where sexual sin is likely to happen, you're just setting yourself up. Each person is different and can handle different levels of access to the person they're attracted to. But honesty about what you cannot handle is necessary to avoid situations where you find yourself doing the very thing you've vowed not to do.

11) I will not allow outside voices to encourage doubt in my belief about God or His ability to fulfill the desires of my heart.

I stopped listening to other single women who had never been married, married people who didn't marry or date God's way, and people who were unhappy in their marriages. I also stopped listening to people who had no compassion for singles who hasn't married by the age of 30. The things they said to me were disheartening at best. And the advice they gave was often ungodly and horrible. Most importantly, it undermined what I was asking God to do— which was to help me maintain my hope while I waited on Him to fulfill a desire of my heart.

12) I will pray for my future husband.

Again, at the end of the day, your ability to cope with and overcome the difficulties of life is impacted by your prayer life. If you're having difficult patches or trying not to fall into desperation, and you find yourself doubting that God has anyone for you, pray. Pray for your future husband in every way you can think of. A great book that helps you to do that is *Praying for Your Future Husband* by Robin Jones Gunn and Tricia Goyer. God wants to hear what you have to say about the matter. And your future husband may need prayer to help him avoid traps that will only delay him even longer.

Answers to Some Common Questions Single Women Ask

Now I want us to have some fun. Here are my answers to some of the most common questions I've either had single women ask me, or that I've heard asked in forums for singles. Enjoy and if you have other questions, ask me here: afi@authoroffaithmin.com.

1) There are more men than women. How do we deal with that?

What's worked best for me and other single women know is prayer. There are many things about dating today that will stress you out and drive you crazy if you allow it. Prayer is not only communication with God, but it's an opportunity for you to turn the problem over to Him. He also speaks back to you, so learn how to recognize His voice. So naturally, He could reveal lessons and strategies on how to deal with this particular problem in a way that's specific to you.

Another way to deal with this is to be open to blind dates set up by people you know and trust. Once you're out of college, you have to be creative about meeting new people, and the easiest way to meet new men who would be a good match for you is to be open to blind dates set up by friends and family who have your best interests at heart.

2) Is it okay to ask a man out or give him my number?

Absolutely…if you're okay with dating and eventually marrying a man who has no aspirations to take on the responsibility of leading a wife and family. As soon as you approach a man and start to pursue him, you set the tone of you being the one who will pursue him throughout the rest of your relationship. Even worse, you'll find yourself constantly doing things to prove your worthiness to him. Remember, marriage-minded men who love God pursue women.

3) How do you know if a man is into you?

He'll tell you. Then his actions will match up with his words. Remember what happened with Adam and Eve after God created Eve? Adam said something like this: "God, finally! Where have you been hiding this woman all my life?" And then he married her. Now, this doesn't mean that every man who's interested in you will want to marry you. It does mean that a man who's interested in you will say it and then show it in his actions. It also means that the man who wants to marry you will say it, and then prove it with his actions. He'll call. He'll show up when he says he will or will call if something beyond his control stops him from keeping his word. He'll spend time with you. He'll spend money on you. It doesn't have to be a lot, but it will always be something thoughtful. He'll introduce you to his friends and family. And when he's ready to make you a part of his life he'll make the necessary arrangements or rearrangements to do so.

4) Why are there so many more women than men in church?

Honestly, I think most churches appeal more to the emotional needs and the spiritual states of women, and often lack strong men's ministries where men can go to talk to and fellowship with strong men. If you've noticed this in your own church, ask your leadership about it and see if they'd be open to starting a men's ministry. Then ask any male friends you have if they would participate. But keep the right motive. Do it so that your brothers in Christ will grow in their relationship with God. Not so that you'll have your pick from a growing pool of Christian men in your church.

5) Why do men marry women who aren't marriage material?

I think they do it for the same reasons that women marry men who aren't marriage material. Lust. Lack of hope. Lack of dating know-how. And there are others. But don't get sucked down the emotional rabbit hole of wondering why this happens. It will make you bitter towards men and feel as though you have to compete with other women.

6) But if you wait until you get married to have sex, how will you know if you're sexually compatible?

Good question. I think you can actually judge by two things: your physical attraction to each other during your dating to courtship relationship, and whether or not he has a teachable spirit. Those two things, combined with knowing that the Holy Spirit is telling you that you two should proceed in a dating to courtship relationship are pretty good indicators of future sexual compatibility. But remember...that's only one part of several things that are needed to keep a lifelong, godly marriage together. Don't focus so much on sex that you forget to consider all the other ways in which you should be compatible.

7) What's the point of waiting until marriage for sex? No one is going to do that!

The point is that it's God's best for you. I used to think it was just God being withholding. But it's God's way of protecting you from the unnecessary heartache that comes with having sex with men who have no intention of marrying you. It's also not true that men won't wait. Maybe all the ones you've met weren't willing. But a man who truly loves you will wait.

8) But I've already had sex outside of marriage. Why does it matter if I adopt celibacy before marriage now?

If you are a woman who is in Christ, God will make you a new creation. Honestly, God's character is that of patience, love, and acceptance. He hates your sin but loves you. And if you have the desire to abstain but feel it doesn't matter, it's a lie that Satan is trying to plant in your mind. God cares. He cares about your sexuality, your desire for marriage, and even your happiness.

9) Where are all the *men*?

Everywhere. Do I think you can go certain places and your chances of meeting men will be increased? Absolutely. But when you're looking for a dating to courtship marriage, going specific places to meet men can be counterproductive. I'm not saying you shouldn't do it, but if you go and don't meet someone or if you do and things don't go the way you want, you have to work through disappointment. And that's hard to do when you truly desire marriage. So the best thing you can do is become active outside of work, church, and the gym. Join a civic organization. Join a safe meetup.com group. Ask your friends to introduce you to new friends and expand your social circle. Be open to going on blind dates when trusted friends and family members set you up. Live your life every single day.

10) I'm highly educated and successful, why is it so hard to meet a man who matches my educational and professional levels of achievement?

Before I answer that, answer these questions. Why do you need to marry a man who has the same exact level of professional and educational achievement as you? Why did you achieve it in the first place?

Now, I know that many women are taught they need to have a man with the same level of achievement. I do not agree. I think what matters more is his character and whether or not he can handle your success. If he has godly character and can handle it, ask him what his plans are for the future. If you agree with his plans, why does it matter if they lead to the same type of achievement as yours? If he has a plan to take care of you regardless of who makes more, what's the problem? I'm not saying to allow a man with no ambition to take advantage of you. By all means, keep yourself out of situations where you're out in the workforce working hard every day while he lives at home making no attempt to match or exceed your efforts. But underneath that desire of wanting your husband to have a certain level of achievement, I think there's a spirit of pride and competition and there's no room for that in a godly, lifelong marriage. It's time to dismantle it, look past net worth, and figure out a man's true worth, which comes from his character and heart.

11) I make more money than the men who ask me out. How do I work that out?

Let's look back at the answer to number 10. Why is it important that your husband makes more money than you? Then consider the ways that a man who makes less money than you can still be a good husband to you and a good father to future children per God's standards. Read Proverbs 31 and the account of Deborah in the book of Judges for a little inspiration!

12) Why is it so hard to find men that meet my standards?

That depends on what your standards are. If they're standards that are unrealistic, that could be why. To me, unrealistic means you have to have a man who is 6'5", makes $250,000 a year, looks like (insert name of favorite male celebrity), drives a (insert name of expensive car), lives in (insert name of expensive neighborhood), has a six-pack, and I could continue on and on. Why on earth would you need that specific combination of things in order to have a happy, lifelong, godly marriage? What happens if he loses his job? Or becomes disfigured due to circumstances beyond his control?

I'm not saying you shouldn't want what you want. But as you mature in God, what you want should mirror more of what God says you need in order to have a happy, lifelong, godly marriage.

13) Why is it so hard to find a good man?

What's your definition of a good man? I've found that many women base their definition of good based on external and/or temporal qualities—not internal or lasting qualities.

They find men who have those temporal qualities, then wonder why the relationship doesn't work out. External/temporal qualities are like this: sexy, good-looking, has an amazing body, muscular, makes $150,000 a year, is a doctor, is a lawyer, drives an expensive car, is a good lover. These are all qualities that don't testify to who he is as a person. Internal and lasting qualities are like this: has a plan for his life, has a relationship with God or is open to building one, has leadership ability, treats people with kindness, works hard, is generous. If you constantly find yourself asking why it's so hard to find a good man, first determine what your definition of a good man is. If you see that definition is based on temporal and external qualities, focus on what internal and lasting qualities you believe you want in a husband.

14) Who should pay on the first date?

I would say it depends on what you're comfortable with. I, however, am old school and feel that if a man is trying to win you over, he won't mind paying. Remember, men who are interested in you and eventually love you will provide for you. And they won't complain about it as long as they feel you appreciate it and reciprocate it.

15) Why do men chase after women that don't love them?

Good question. I've often wondered the same thing myself. My answer is three-fold. First, I suspect it has something to do with the fact that when we love and are in love with someone, we go out of our way for them and make it easy for them to have access to us. Remember, men generally like to be challenged. And if you're giving up too much too soon, you could be losing the attention of men who like you but feel you're "too easy" to win over. So you could be lacking in or just need to brush up on your interpersonal skills in romantic relationships.

Second, I mostly feel that men who like women who constantly give them that type of challenge like to play games. I've met men who say they need a woman who can always challenge them. Although I never dated a man like this, just interacting with them left me drained. They were always trying to show me some game, interrupt me while I was answering a question they asked, or point out the flaws in my "argument" (silly me, I thought we were having a conversation, not a debate). I personally don't have the energy for that. If I have to always come up with ways to keep you entertained, I'm not interested. So it could just be that he has a short attention span and needs someone who's willing to keep him entertained 24/7.

Third, if you find that the men you're attracted to are interested in women who don't seem to love them, you might be focused on the wrong type of man. Maybe you need a man who appreciates that you demand respect but also loves the fact that you don't play games. He might actually like that while you're steady, consistent, and have standards, you don't make it difficult for him to get to know you. There are plenty of men like this. They like to be direct, they like to pursue and they don't play games. So pay attention to all the different types of men you meet. Not just the ones you like who are are going after women you don't approve of.

16) Why does what I wear and look like matter?

Not that women don't like handsome men, but men are just wired to be moved by what they see. Think about it this way: If you were presented with two diamonds of the same quality but one was in a carefully sculpted and expensive box while the other was in a plastic shopping bag, wouldn't you question why the owner chose to put a diamond in a plastic shopping bag? Here's another example...would you eat steak off a trash can lid? As much as people hate to admit it, presentation matters. So just think about clothes, accessories, and self-care regimens that make you feel good and you won't go wrong.

My dear sister in Christ, it was a joy to share the lessons God has taught me during my hardest season of singleness. I truly believe that God is in the business of matchmaking and that if you want a lifelong, godly marriage, He is the best in the "business"!

If you need weekly encouragement, make sure to join me at authorofmyfaith.com/blog and follow me there. Also, you can go to http://www.authorofmyfaith.com/letstalkcommunity and join the "Let's Talk About It" Community for a safe place to talk about your dating and relationship challenges.

If you enjoyed this book, check out these other resources at my e-store:

www.e-junkie.com/authoroffaith

Back To Basics
EASY TIPS ON HOW TO JUMPSTART YOUR RELATIONSHIP WITH GOD

BY AFI PITTMAN

Breaking Soul Ties

BREAKING SOUL TIES TO EVERY MR. WRONG SO YOU CAN MEET MR. RIGHT

BY AFI PITTMAN

www.ingramcontent.com/pod-product-compliance
Lightning Source LLC
Chambersburg PA
CBHW070806050426
42452CB00011B/1911